Agile Swift

Swift Programming Using
Agile Tools and Techniques

Godfrey Nolan

Apress®

Agile Swift: Swift Programming Using Agile Tools and Techniques

Godfrey Nolan
Huntington Woods, Michigan, USA

ISBN-13 (pbk): 978-1-4842-2101-3   ISBN-13 (electronic): 978-1-4842-2102-0
10.1007/978-1-4842-2102-0

Library of Congress Control Number: 2016961810

Managing Director: Welmoed Spahr
Lead Editor: Aaron Black
Technical Reviewer: Bruce Wade
Editorial Board: Steve Anglin, Pramila Balan, Laura Berendson, Aaron Black, Louise Corrigan, Jonathan Gennick, Robert Hutchinson, Celestin Suresh John, Nikhil Karkal, James Markham, Susan McDermott, Matthew Moodie, Natalie Pao, Gwenan Spearing
Coordinating Editor: Jessica Vakili
Copy Editor: Kezia Endsley
Compositor: SPi Global
Indexer: SPi Global
Artist: SPi Global

Distributed to the book trade worldwide by Springer Science+Business Media New York, 233 Spring Street, 6th Floor, New York, NY 10013. Phone 1-800-SPRINGER, fax (201) 348-4505, e-mail orders-ny@springer-sbm.com, or visit www.springeronline.com. Apress Media, LLC is a California LLC and the sole member (owner) is Springer Science + Business Media Finance Inc (SSBM Finance Inc). SSBM Finance Inc is a **Delaware** corporation.

For information on translations, please e-mail rights@apress.com, or visit www.apress.com.

Apress and friends of ED books may be purchased in bulk for academic, corporate, or promotional use. eBook versions and licenses are also available for most titles. For more information, reference our Special Bulk Sales–eBook Licensing web page at www.apress.com/bulk-sales.

Any source code or other supplementary materials referenced by the author in this text are available to readers at www.apress.com. For detailed information about how to locate your book's source code, go to www.apress.com/source-code/. Readers can also access source code at SpringerLink in the Supplementary Material section for each chapter.

Printed on acid-free paper

Contents at a Glance

Contents

About the Author

Godfrey Nolan is founder and president of RIIS LLC, a mobile development firm in the Detroit Metro area. He is also the author of *Agile Android, Bulletproof Android, Android Best Practices, Decompiling Android,* and *Decompiling Java.* Godfrey has spoken at DroidCon and AnDevCon, as well as JavaOne, ASP-Connections, VSLive, CodeMash, Code PaLOUsa, 1DevDay, and many local Java and .NET user groups on a wide range of topics such as continuous integration, executable requirements, and mobile security.

About the Technical Reviewer

Bruce Wade is a software engineer from British Columbia, Canada. He started in software development when he was 16 years old by coding his first web site. He went on to study computer information systems at DeVry Institute of Technology in Calgary, then to further enhance his skills, he studied visual and game programming at The Art Institute, Vancouver. Over the years, he has worked for large corporations as well as for several start-ups. His software experience led him to utilize many technologies, including C/C++, Python, Objective-C, Swift, Postgres, and JavaScript. In 2012 he started the company, Warply Designed, to focus on mobile 2D/3D and OS X development. Aside from hacking out new ideas, he enjoys spending time hiking with his Boxer Rasco, working out, and exploring new adventures.

CHAPTER 1

Introduction

Swift was announced at the WWDC in 2014 and surprisingly in 2015 the code was open sourced. It can run on both OSX and Ubuntu, which is a huge departure for Apple, which has typically been a more closed system. The Swift language is a completely different animal than Objective-C.

Being new, it doesn't have many of the arcane aspects of the much older Objective-C. Its learning curve is much shallower than Objective-C and will allow new developers to quickly crank out iOS apps. Well, that is Apple's plan anyway.

Although very new, Swift is evolving quickly and already has built-in unit testing using XCTest and UI testing using XCUI. As an introduction to Swift Agile testing, we're going to look at how to do a simple unit test written in Swift, both in Xcode and on the Ubuntu Linux platform. We'll finish by writing a UI test using the new XCUI API testing framework.

Hello World Unit Test

Before we go any further let's look at a simple unit test. For demonstration purposes we can use a simple Hello World example, which can be created by typing `swift package init` on the command line. See Listing 1-1.

Listing 1-1. Hello World

```
struct HelloWorld {
    var text = "Hello, World!"
}
```

The corresponding unit test is shown in Listing 1-2, which tests whether the text variable is "Hello, World!" or not.

Listing 1-2. Hello World Unit Test

```
func testExample() {
    XCTAssertEqual(HelloWorld().text, "Hello, World!")
}
```

G. Nolan, *Agile Swift*, DOI 10.1007/978-1-4842-2102-0_1

Unit tests use assertions to make sure the method provides the expected result. In this case, we're using XCTAssertEqual to see if the Add method returns 2 when adding 1 + 1. If the test works, then we should see the output shown in Listing 1-3 when we run the swift test command.

Listing 1-3. Test output

```
$ swift test
Test Suite 'All tests' started at 13:12:28.961
Test Suite 'debug.xctest' started at 13:12:28.976
Test Suite 'HelloWorldTests' started at 13:12:28.976
Test Case 'HelloWorldTests.testExample' started at 13:12:28.976
Test Case 'HelloWorldTests.testExample' passed (0.0 seconds).
Test Suite 'HelloWorldTests' passed at 13:12:28.976
        Executed 1 test, with 0 failures (0 unexpected) in 0.0 (0.0)
        seconds
Test Suite 'debug.xctest' passed at 13:12:28.976
        Executed 1 test, with 0 failures (0 unexpected) in 0.0 (0.0)
        seconds
Test Suite 'All tests' passed at 13:12:28.976
        Executed 1 test, with 0 failures (0 unexpected) in 0.0 (0.0)
        seconds
```

Benefits

If you're new to Agile development, you're probably wondering how Agile can improve the development process. At its most basic, Agile and unit testing in particular helps with the following:

- Catch more mistakes
- Confidently make more changes
- Perform built-in regression testing
- Extend the life of your codebase

If you write unit tests and they cover a significant portion of your code, then you're going to catch more bugs. You can make simple changes to tidy up the code or make extensive architectural changes. If you run your unit tests after your changes and they all pass then you can be confident that you didn't introduce any subtle defects.

The more unit tests you write, the more you can regression test your app whenever you change the code. And once you have a lot of unit tests then it becomes a regression test suite that allows you to have the confidence to do things you wouldn't otherwise attempt.

Unit tests mean you no longer have to program with a "leave well enough alone" mindset. You can now make significant changes, such as changing to a new database, updating your backend API, and even changing from Objective-C to Swift, and be happy that your app is behaving the same as before you made the changes if all the tests execute without any errors.

Agile Testing Pyramid

There are several types of tests you need in your test suite to make sure your app is fully tested. You should have unit tests for the component or method level functionality, API tests for any backend, RESTful APIs and GUI tests for your iOS screens, and general application workflow.

The classic Agile test pyramid first appeared in Mike Cohn's book *Succeeding with Agile*. This pyramid is a good guide of the relative quantity of each type of tests your app is going to need; see Figure 1-1.

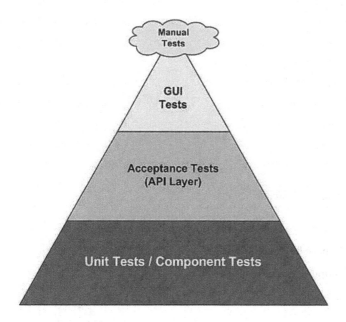

Figure 1-1. *Agile pyramid*

In this book we're going to focus primarily on unit tests as well as some GUI tests. We'll begin by showing how to create a simple unit test in both flavors of Swift—Ubuntu and Xcode—as well as a simple GUI test using XCUI.

Calculator Unit Tests in Xcode

In the following example we show how to create a simple calculator in Xcode. It's not even a true calculator, as it just adds two numbers. See Figure 1-2. This unit test should return true assuming adding two numbers in the app works correctly.

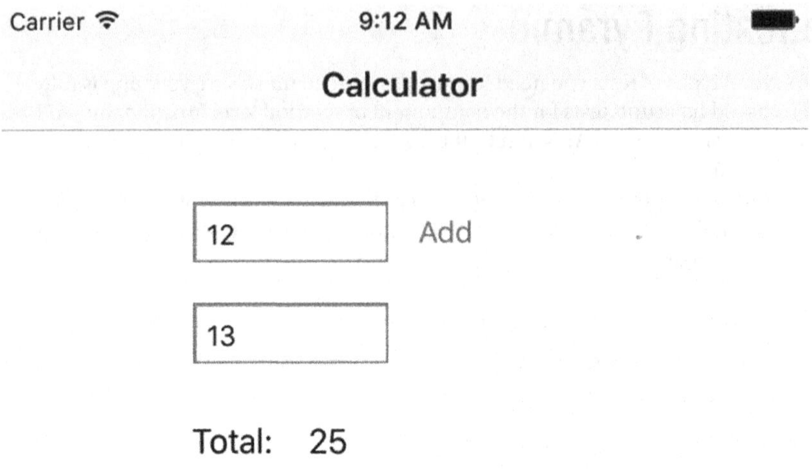

Carrier 📶   9:12 AM

Calculator

12   Add

13

Total: 25

Figure 1-2. Adding two numbers in Xcode

To set up and run a unit test, you need to perform the following tasks:

- Make sure you have the prerequisites
- Create and compile calculator code
- Create unit test code
- Run unit tests

Prerequisites

The minimum requirements for the Swift examples in this book are OSX 10.11 (El Capitan) and Xcode 8.0. The following example was created using Xcode 8.0 with Swift 3.0 running on OSX 10.11.

Getting Started

1. In Xcode, choose File ➤ New Project and then choose an iOS single view application. See Figure 1-3.

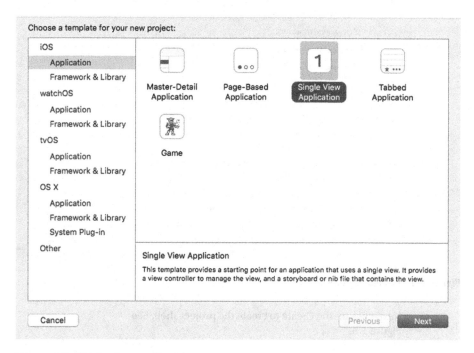

Figure 1-3. *Single view application*

2. Click Next. Then choose Calculator as the Product Name. Choose Swift as the language and check the Include Unit Tests and Include UI Test checkboxes. See Figure 1-4.

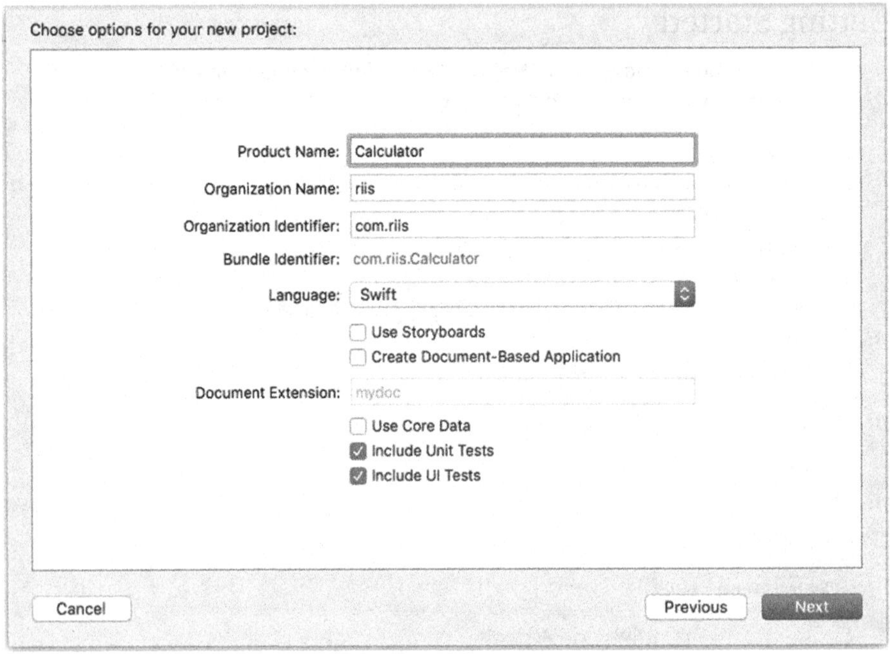

Choose options for your new project:

Product Name:	Calculator
Organization Name:	riis
Organization Identifier:	com.riis
Bundle Identifier:	com.riis.Calculator
Language:	Swift

☐ Use Storyboards
☐ Create Document-Based Application

Document Extension: mydoc

☐ Use Core Data
☑ Include Unit Tests
☑ Include UI Tests

Cancel   Previous   Next

Figure 1-4. *Project options*

3.   Next, click on the Create to create the project shell. See
      Figure 1-5.

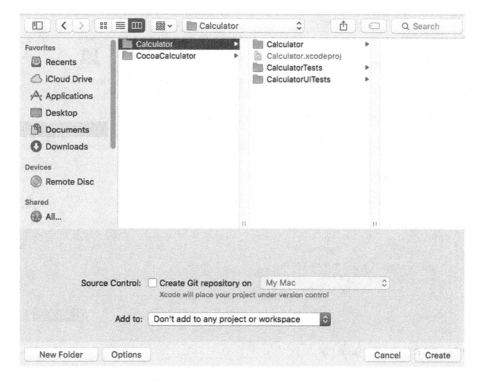

Figure 1-5. *Create an application*

Creating a Class

Now we need to add the calculator's code, as follows.

1. Choose File ➤ New ➤ File and then choose Swift File as the
   template for your file, as shown in Figure 1-6.

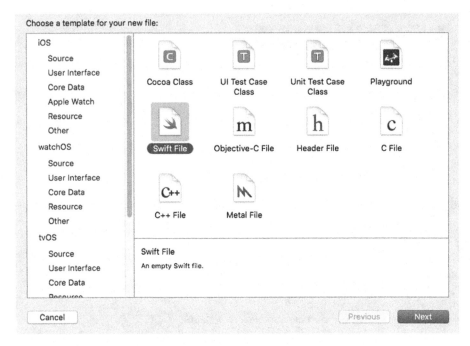

Figure 1-6. *Create a Swift file*

2. Name the file `CalculatorModel.swift`; see Figure 1-7.

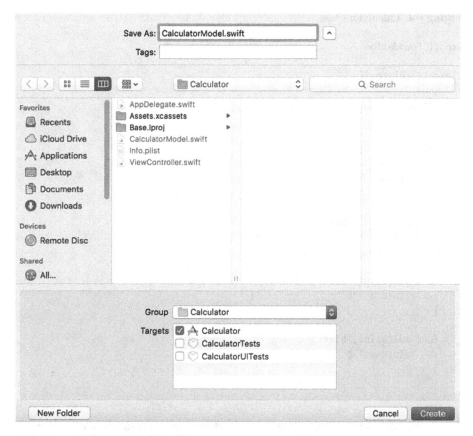

Figure 1-7. *CalculatorModel.swift*

3. Add the Calculator class code to CalculatorModel.swift, as shown in Listing 1-4.

Listing 1-4. Calculator Class

```
import Foundation

class Calculator {

    var a: Int
    var b: Int

    init(a:Int, b:Int){
        self.a = a
        self.b = b
    }

    func add(a:Int, b:Int) -> Int {
        return a + b
    }

    func sub(a:Int, b:Int) -> Int {
        return a - b
    }

    func mul(a:Int, b:Int) -> Int {
        return a * b
    }

}
```

To simplify our testing we're initializing the class so we can prefill the data in the two fields that we're going to add. We've also added some other functions that we'll use later.

Setting Up the User Interface

Next we need to create the user interface in Xcode so we can add our two numbers on an iOS device.

1. In the Project Navigator, click on the Main.storyboard file

2. Search for Text Field in the Object Library ◎.

3. Drag two text fields onto the View Controller in the Storyboard.

4. Search for Button in the Object Library ◎.

5. Drag a button and place it beside the two text fields.

6. Double-click on the button and change its text to Add.

7. Search for a Label in the Object Library ⊚

8. Drag two labels on to the View Controller and place them under the text fields.

9. Click on the Label and rename one to Total: and the other to Result.

When you're finished, the View Controller should look like Figure 1-8.

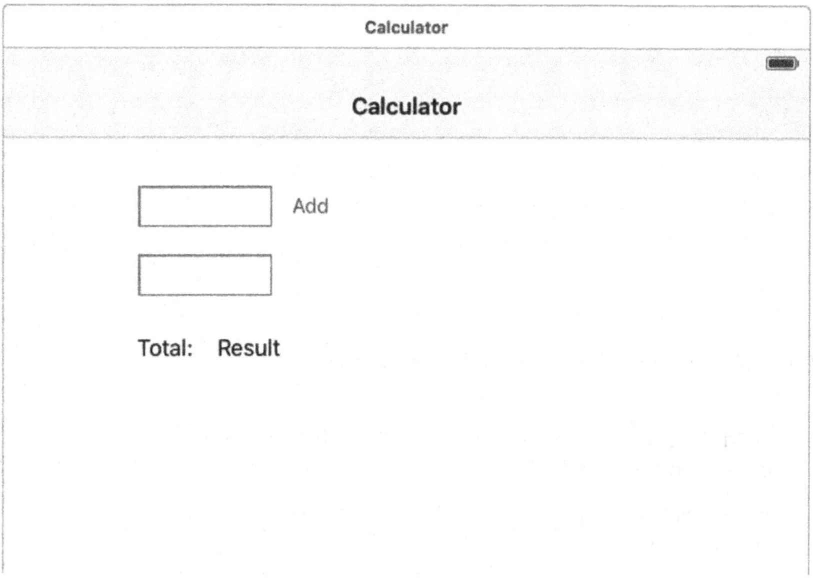

Figure 1-8. Calculator Storyboard

Setting Up the Outlets

To connect the elements on our View Controller to the code, we need to first set up our outlets.

1. We want to make some room to show the ViewController and the swift code, so first click on ▢ to hide the Document Outline.

2. Click on Show the Assistant Window ⊘ to see the View Controller code.

3. It's still crowded, so click on ▢ to hide the Utility area of Xcode. See Figure 1-9.

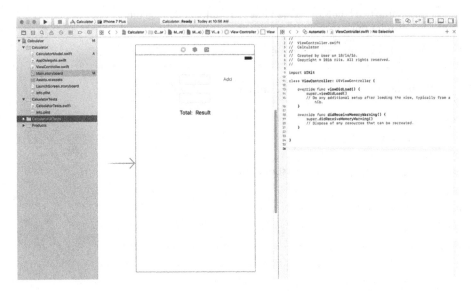

Figure 1-9. *Calculator Storyboard and View Controller code*

4. Hold Ctrl and drag from the first text field to just under the class definition.

5. In the menu that pops up, choose the following (see Figure 1-10) and click Connect.

- Connection: Outlet

- Name: aTextField

- Type: UITextField

- Storage: Weak

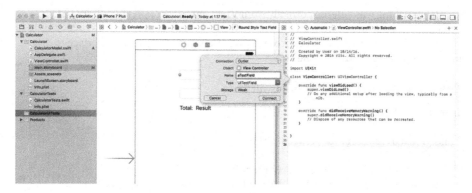

Figure 1-10. *IBOutlet for aTextField*

6. Repeat these steps for bTextField.

7. Hold Ctrl and drag from the Result Label to just under the class definition.

8. In the menu that pops up, choose the following

   • Connection: Outlet

   • Name: resultLabel

   • Type: UILabel

   • Storage: Weak

9. Now let's create an IBAction for the Add button so it can call a method to add the values in the text field values and put the result in the resultField.

10. Click on the Add button and, while holding the Ctrl button, drag it to the space under the IBOutlets.

11. In the pop-up menu, choose the following:

    • Connection: Action

    • Name: calculateTapped

    • Type: UIButton

    • Event: Touch Up Inside

    • Arguments: Sender

12. Click Connect.

If everything was entered correctly, your ViewController.swift code should be similar to the code in Listing 1-5.

Listing 1-5 shows the ViewController.swift code that allows our interface to interact with the CalculatorModel class.

Listing 1-5. Updated ViewController.swift Code

```swift
import UIKit

class ViewController: UIViewController {

    @IBOutlet var aTextField : UITextField!
    @IBOutlet var bTextField : UITextField!
    @IBOutlet var resultLabel : UILabel!

    @IBAction func calculateTapped(_ sender : UIButton) {
    }

    override func viewDidLoad() {
        super.viewDidLoad()
    }

    override func didReceiveMemoryWarning() {
        super.didReceiveMemoryWarning()
    }

}
```

In Listing 1-5, we can see the IBOutlet definitions for the two text fields and the result label where we're going to put the result of our calculation. We also have an IBAction that will call the Calculator.Add method and update the resultLable field.

To finish our simplest addition calculator, we need to create a calculator object resCalc = Calculator() and update the resultLabel so it adds aTextField and bTextField. This code is shown in Listing 1-6.

Listing 1-6. Updated calculateTapped() Method

```swift
let resCalc = Calculator(a:0, b:0)

@IBAction func calculateTapped(_ sender: UIButton) {
  resultLabel.text =
    String(resCalc.add(
        a: Int((aTextField.text! as NSString).intValue),
        b: Int((bTextField.text! as NSString).intValue)))

}
```

Run the app and click the Add button to make sure that the calculation is working correctly.

Create Unit Test Code

Add the code in Listing 1-7 to the CalculatorTests.swift file, which you'll find in the CalculatorTests directory created by Xcode.

Listing 1-7. CalculatorTests.swift

```
import XCTest
@testable import Calculator

class CalculatorTests: XCTestCase {

    let resCalc = Calculator(a:0, b:0)

    override func setUp() {
        super.setUp()
    }

    override func tearDown() {
        super.tearDown()
    }

    func testAdd() {
        XCTAssertEqual(resCalc.add(a: 1,b: 1),2)
        XCTAssertEqual(resCalc.add(a: 1,b: 2),3)
        XCTAssertEqual(resCalc.add(a: 5,b: 4),9)
    }

}
```

CalculatorTests imports the calculator code and the XCTest framework. After initializing the calc object, we have a testAdd method to test some simple calculations using the XCTAssertEqual assertions. We assert that 1+1 is equal to 2, 1+2 is 3, and 5+4 is 9.

Run Unit Tests

To run the tests, click on the Test navigator tab (5th) to see Figure 1-11.

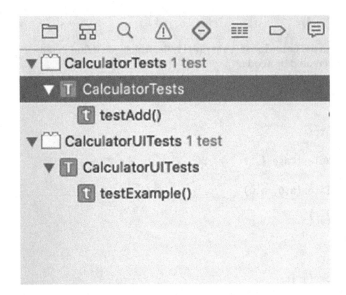

Figure 1-11. *Test navigator*

Right-click on CalculatorTests and choose Run CalculatorTests. If the tests pass, you should see a green checkmark beside the test method showing it passed. See Figure 1-12.

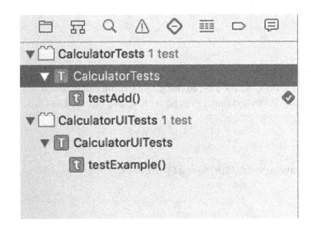

Figure 1-12. *Passing tests*

If the tests don't pass, it'll show up a red X with the offending XCTAssertEqual highlighted; see Figure 1-13.

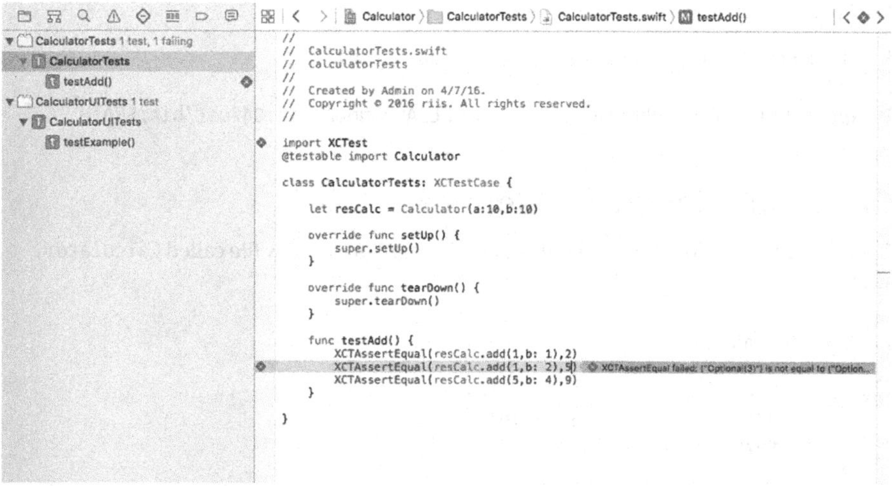

Figure 1-13. *Failing the test*

Hello World Unit Test in Ubuntu

In the following example, we show how to create our simple unit test example on the Ubuntu platform. This should also return true, assuming adding two numbers in the calculator Android app works correctly.

I'm also going to contradict what I said earlier about Swift, as unit tests on Ubuntu are the one area where Swift is not very smooth or obvious. So it needs some explanation before it gets fixed in later versions of Swift. We'll talk about that more in the Ubuntu tweaks section.

To set up and run a unit test, we need to talk about the following steps:

- Install the prerequisites

- Create and compile the calculator code

- Create the test code

- Add Ubuntu tweaks

- Run the unit tests

Prerequisites

You need to be using either Ubuntu 14.04 or 15.10. Download the latest 3.x development snapshot from https://swift.org/download/. This is a ZIP file with the compiled Swift binaries so you can unzip it and add it to your path as shown in Listing 1-8. Modify your snapshot name appropriately.

Listing 1-8. Creating a Swift Environment

```
$ tar -xvzf swift-3.0-RELEASE-ubuntu14.04.tar.gz
$ pwd
$ export PATH=/home/ubuntu/swift-3.0-RELEASE-ubuntu14.04/usr/bin:$PATH
```

Create and Compile Code

Create a sources folder and add the code in Listing 1-9 to a new file called `Calculator.swift`.

Listing 1-9. Calculator.swift

```
class Calculator {
    func add(a:Int, _ b:Int) -> Int {
        return a + b
    }

    func sub(a:Int, _ b:Int) -> Int {
        return a - b
    }

    func mul(a:Int, _ b:Int) -> Int {
        return a * b
    }
}
```

Before we compile the code, we need to create a Package Manager file in the top-level directory; see `Package.swift` in Listing 1-10.

Listing 1-10. Package.swift

```
import PackageDescription

let package = Package(
    name: "Calculator"
)
```

If everything is set up correctly, you should have the structure shown in Figure 1-14.

```
├── Package.swift
└── Sources
        └── Calulator.swift

1 directory, 2 files
```

Figure 1-14. *Initial directory structure*

Run the swift build command, which will create a .build directory if the code compiles.

Create Test Code

Create a Tests directory and enter the code in Listing 1-11 into a new file called CalculatorTests.swift, which you should put in the Tests/CalculatorTests directory.

Listing 1-11. CalculatorTests.swift

```
import XCTest
@testable import Calculator

class CalculatorTests: XCTestCase {
  var calc : Calculator!

  override func setUp() {
    super.setUp()
    calc = Calculator()
  }

  func testAddCheck() {
    XCTAssertEqual(calc.add(1,1),2)
  }
}
```

CalculatorTests imports the calculator code and the XCTest framework. We have a setup that initializes the calc object and a test method to check that 1 + 1 does indeed equal 2.

Ubuntu Tweaks

In Xcode the code in Listing 1-11 would work fine, but we need a few extras in Ubuntu. First create a LinuxMain.swift file in the Tests directory. It creates the constructor for the tests, as shown in Listing 1-12.

Listing 1-12. LinuxMain.swift

```
import XCTest
@testable import CalculatorTests

XCTMain([
    testCase(CalculatorTests.allTests)
])
```

Finally, we also need to add some XCTest extensions to the test case in CalculatorTests.swift that lists all our tests methods. See Listing 1-13.

Listing 1-13. XCTest Extension

```
extension CalculatorTests {
    static var allTests : [(String, (CalculatorTests) -> () throws -> Void)]
{
        return [
            ("testAddCheck", testAddCheck)
        ]
    }
}
```

Figure 1-15 shows the directory structure for our code and tests.

```
├── Package.swift
├── Sources
│   └── Calulator.swift
└── Tests
        ├── Calculator
        │   └── CalculatorTests.swift
        └── LinuxMain.swift
```

3 directories, 4 files

Figure 1-15. *Project directory structure*

Run Unit Tests

Run the `swift test` command to see the result of the unit tests. If your tests are successful they show the output shown in Listing 1-14.

Listing 1-14. Command-Line Unit Test Output on Ubuntu

```
$ swift test
Test Suite 'All tests' started at 13:12:28.961
Test Suite 'debug.xctest' started at 13:12:28.976
Test Suite 'HelloWorldTests' started at 13:12:28.976
Test Case 'HelloWorldTests.testExample' started at 13:12:28.976
Test Case 'HelloWorldTests.testExample' passed (0.0 seconds).
Test Suite 'HelloWorldTests' passed at 13:12:28.976
        Executed 1 test, with 0 failures (0 unexpected) in 0.0 (0.0) seconds
Test Suite 'debug.xctest' passed at 13:12:28.976
        Executed 1 test, with 0 failures (0 unexpected) in 0.0 (0.0) seconds
Test Suite 'All tests' passed at 13:12:28.976
        Executed 1 test, with 0 failures (0 unexpected) in 0.0 (0.0) seconds
```

GUI Tests

If we look back at the Agile pyramid, we can see that we also need some GUI tests. We can use the XCUI API framework for our testing. XCUI was released at WWDC 2015 and is short for XCTest and UI. In XCUI we have a choice. We can either write the code from scratch or record interactions with the UI and then modify the code later.

■ **Note** You can only do GUI tests in Xcode. You can't do any XCUI testing on the Ubuntu platform as the open source version of Swift is missing all of the UIKit GUI classes.

Hello World GUI Test

Listing 1-15 shows a simple example where we launch the previous calculator app, as shown in Figure 1-8.

To create an XCUI test, do the following:

1. Click on CalculatorUITests in the `CalculatorUITests` folder.

2. Click within the `testExample()` method

3. Click the red record button, which is highlighted in Figure 1-16.

4. Enter 12 in the first text field

5. Enter 13 in the second text field

6. Click the Add button, which will update the Result field to 25.

7. Click on the Result field.

```
29        ʃ
30
31        func testExample() {
32
33
34            // Use recording to get started writing UI tests.
35            // Use XCTAssert and related functions to verify your tests produce th
36        }
37
38    }
39
```

Figure 1-16. XCUI record button

The generated code can be seen in Listing 1-15.

Listing 1-15. GUI Tests

```
import XCTest

class CalculatorUITests: XCTestCase {

    override func setUp() {
        super.setUp()
        XCUIApplication().launch()

    }

    func testExample() {
        let app = XCUIApplication()
        let addElementsQuery = app.otherElements.containing(.button,
        identifier:"Add")
        let textField = addElementsQuery.children(matching: .textField).
        element(boundBy: 0)
        textField.tap()
        textField.typeText("12")

        let textField2 = addElementsQuery.children(matching: .textField).
        element(boundBy: 1)
        textField2.tap()
        textField2.typeText("13")
        app.buttons["Add"].tap()

        XCTAssert(app.staticTexts["25"].exists)     }

}
```

The text fields in our sample app are 12 and 13, so if everything is working correctly, the Result label will display 25. tap() simulates a user clicking on the Add button and XCTAssert's that 25 is displayed. See Figure 1-17.

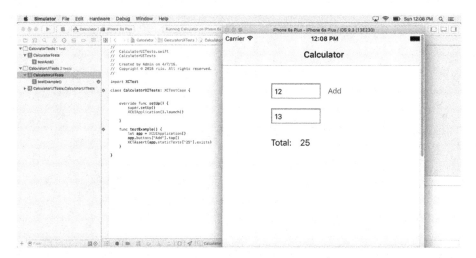

Figure 1-17. *Running the XCUI tests*

Right-click on the calculator tests and choose Run Calculator Tests to run the GUI tests. The Xcode simulator fires and the test code interacts with the GUI and passes or fails, depending on your tests.

Summary

In this chapter, we looked at an overview of the current state of Swift unit testing and UI testing in Xcode and on the Ubuntu platform. In the rest of the book, we'll explore Agile testing in a lot more detail so you can see how to apply these techniques to your application to produce cleaner, faster code with fewer defects.

## CHAPTER 2

Swift Unit Testing

Swift's implementation of unit testing uses the XCTest library. Swift does not use OCUnit for any unit testing. XCTest is easy to set up and works within Xcode, on the command line in OSX, or on the open source Linux version of Swift.

In this chapter we take a deeper look at Swift unit testing. Unit tests are typically written by developers and not QA folks. Ideally, they're written before or while the application code is being written in a test driven development environment. Writing unit tests weeks after coding, when you've forgotten all about the functionality of the app or the overall context of the code's expected functionality, can be problematic.

Types of Assertions

In our Hello, World and Calculator examples in the last chapter, we used XCTAssertEqual but there are other assertions we can use in the XCTest library. Table 2-1 shows the complete list.

Table 2-1. *Assertions*

Assertion	Description
XCTAssert	Tests that two values are the same
XCTAssertEqual	Tests that two values are equal
XCTAssertEqualWithAccuracy	Tests that two floating point values (a,b) are equal within a tolerance of c
XCTAssertFalse	Tests if a Boolean condition is false
XCTAssertTrue	Tests if a Boolean condition is true
XCTAssertGreaterThan	Tests that one value is greater than the other
XCTAssertGreaterThanOrEqual	Tests that one value is greater or equal to the other
XCTAssertLessThan	Tests that one value is less than the other
XCTAssertLessThanOrEqual	Tests that one value is less than or equal to the other
XCTAssertNil	Tests that an object is nil
XCTAssertNotEqual	Tests that two values are not equal
XCTAssertNotEqualWithAccuracy	Tests that two floating point values (a,b) are not equal within a tolerance of c
XCTAssertNotNil	Tests that an object is not nil

Let's look at some simple examples of these assertions.
XCTAssert(2+2==4,"error message")
XCTAssertEqual(2+2, 4,"error message")
XCTAssertEqualWithAccuracy(5/2, 2.5,0.01,"error message")
XCTAssertFalse(2 == 1,"error message")
XCTAssertTrue(1 == 1)
XCTAssertGreaterThan(2, 1,"error message")
XCTAssertGreaterThanOrEqual(2, 2,"error message")
XCTAssertLessThan(1, 2,"error message")
XCTAssertLessThanOrEqual(1, 2,"error message")
XCTAssertNil(Calculator,"error message")
XCTAssertNotEqual(1, 2,"error message")
XCTAssertNotEqualWithAccuracy(1, 2, 0.1, "error message")
XCTAssertNotNil(Calculator,"error message")

XCTest Options

The XCTest methods always start with the word "test" and then a camel case description of what you are testing, e.g., testDivideByZerosGuarded. It takes no arguments and returns no result. Unit tests live in their own test directory and so do not comingle with the application code. They do not test the user interface or view, but use assertions to test your model code. We will test the view code but it will be in a later chapter using the XCUI library.

The structure of a test file is shown in Listing 2-1, where all test classes are subclasses of XCTestCase.

Listing 2-1. Test Class Structure

```swift
class Tests: XCTestCase {
    override func setUp() {
        // initialization or setup
    }

    func testExample() {
        // assert and verify
    }

    override func tearDown() {
        // revert to original state
    }
}
```

No matter whether you are writing code in Swift, Objective-C, Java, or C#, all unit testing should use the concept of setup-record-verify. Setup means creating objects, data, or even rows in a database so you can simulate the real-world environment. Record means calling the method or object and verify means making sure the test returned the correct results, in our case using assertions. There's also a cleanup task so you can revert the system to how it was before testing started. If you can't easily set up, record, and verify your tests, then unit testing becomes very difficult.

The following XCTest elements help set up, record, and verify your tests.

- @testable
- setUp
- tearDown
- measureBlock

@testable allows us to easily target modules for testing. setUp gets called before each test runs. tearDown gets called after each test runs. And finally, measureBlock provides us with a way to measure how long a test case takes to run.

We'll see later how these are created for us automatically by Xcode. We'll also see later why these are important is helping us organize our tests. Test code should be treated just like real code. It's very easy to start to see test code as having a lower status than your application code. But, just like with your production code, you should be looking at your tests and refactoring them to see if you can make the code neat and tidy so that you or any other developer can understand it at a later date.

@testable

One of the best received Swift 2 features was the introduction of the `@testable` keyword or annotation. This added the ability to access anything internal or public from test cases by making it `@testable`. Now all you need to do is import your model code in your test class and you are good to go. In Figure 2-1, we create the `CalculatorModel.swift` code.

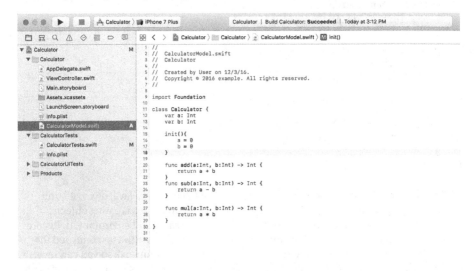

Figure 2-1. *CalculatorModel.swift internal class*

Now we can import the class using the `@testable` keyword, as shown in Figure 2-2. And we can now call the Calculator code and use it in our assertions.

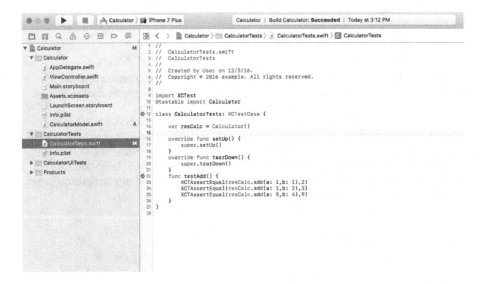

Figure 2-2. *Calculator tests*

setUp

The setup method is used to initialize any data or objects before a test is called. For example, setup could include code to write to log files or create objects to be used in the test. setUp() saves you from having to repeat the calls in each test.

Listing 2-2 shows the test code on Ubuntu without using setUp.

Listing 2-2. Without setUp

```
class Tests: XCTestCase {
  var simpleCalc : Calculator!

  func testAddTwoNumbersCheck() {
    simpleCalc = Calculator()
    XCTAssertEqual(simpleCalc.add(a:1, b:1),2)
  }

  func testSubTwoNumbersCheck() {
    simpleCalc = Calculator()
    XCTAssertEqual(simpleCalc.sub(a:3, b:1),2)
  }

  func testMulTwoNumbersCheck() {
    simpleCalc = Calculator()
    XCTAssertEqual(simpleCalc.mul(a:2, b:3),6)
  }
}
```

Listing 2-3 shows the same test code with the setup() method.

Listing 2-3. With the setUp Method

```
class Tests: XCTestCase {
  var simpleCalc : Calculator!

  override func setUp() {
    super.setUp()
    simpleCalc = Calculator()
  }

  func testAddTwoNumbersCheck() {
    XCTAssertEqual(simpleCalc.add(1,1),2)
  }

  func testSubTwoNumbersCheck() {
    XCTAssertEqual(simpleCalc.sub(3,1),2)
  }
```

```
func testMulTwoNumbersCheck() {
  XCTAssertEqual(simpleCalc.mul(2,3),6)
}
}
```

tearDown

tearDown is called after each test run. Using our previous example, the code becomes Listing 2-4 and the Calculator object is now destroyed before each test method.

Listing 2-4. tearDown

```
class Tests: XCTestCase {
  var simpleCalc : Calculator!

  override func setUp() {
    super.setUp()
    simpleCalc = Calculator()
  }

  override func tearDown() {
    super.tearDown()
    simpleCalc = nil
  }
  func testAddTwoNumbersCheck() {
    XCTAssertEqual(simpleCalc.add(1,1),2)
  }

  func testSubTwoNumbersCheck() {
    XCTAssertEqual(simpleCalc.sub(3,1),2)
  }

  func testMulTwoNumbersCheck() {
    XCTAssertEqual(simpleCalc.mul(2,3),6)
  }
}
```

Performance Testing

Using the `self.measure()` XCTest function, we can see how long a specific test or tests are taking to run. Listing 2-5 shows an example method called `testPerformanceExample()`, which uses `self.measure()` to see how long our XCTAssert on a simple addition would take.

Listing 2-5. Timing Example

```
func testPerformanceExample() {
    self.measure() {
        XCTAssertEqual(self.resCalc.add(a:1, b:2),3)
    }
}
```

If we run the test in Xcode, as shown in Figure 2-3, we also see that the test runs successfully.

Figure 2-3. *Timing your tests*

Additionally, Xcode provides the ability to baseline your test, as shown in Figure 2-4, so that you can see how your test is performing over time to see if it's getting better or worse.

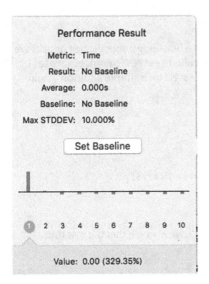

Figure 2-4. Baseline your test times

Calculator App

In this section, we're going to create a simple app to show how easy it is to add unit testing to Swift apps in Xcode. We'll look at how much we get out of the box and then create a calculator app to do some basic unit tests.

First create a new Xcode project. We want it to be a single view (iOS) application. Call it `Calculator` again and make sure to check the Include Unit Tests checkbox (see Figure 2-5).

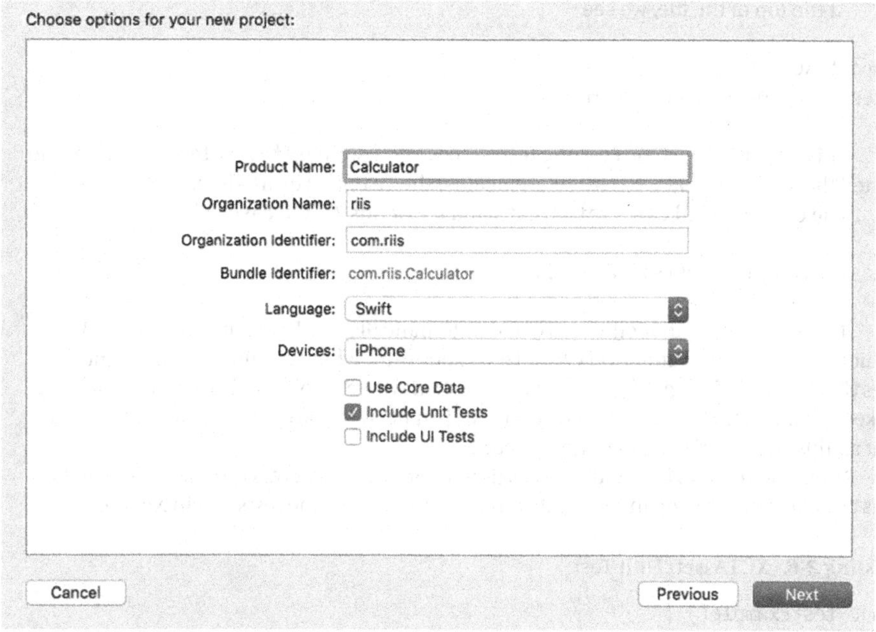

Figure 2-5. *Create application*

Click on the `CalculatorTests` directory once the Xcode editor opens. You should be able to see that the shell of a test file, called `CalculatorTests.swift`, has already been created, as shown in Figure 2-6.

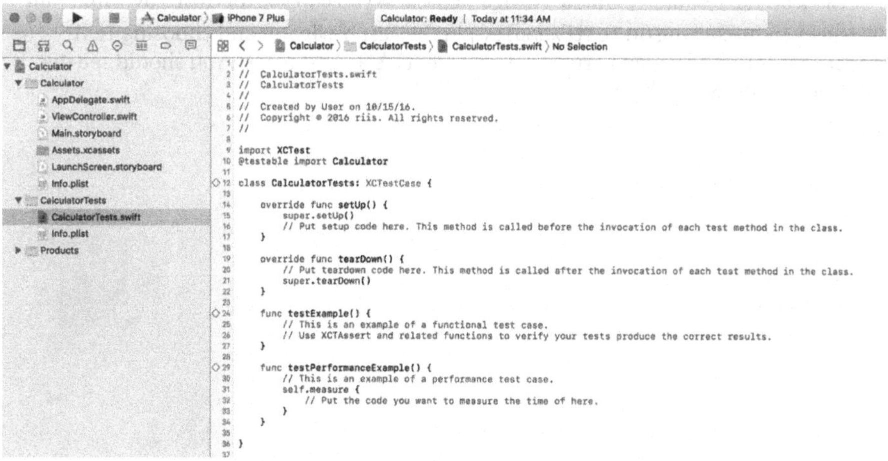

Figure 2-6. *CalculatorTests.swift*

At the top of the file, we see

```
import XCTest
@testable import Calculator
```

This imports the XCTest testing framework and uses the @testable Swift command to tell the compiler that we want to test against the Calculator module.

The class is called CalculatorTests and it extends XCTestCase:

```
class CalculatorTests: XCTestCase
```

There are four stub methods created automatically—setUp() and tearDown(), which run before and after every test, testExample(), which is a unit test stub, and testPerformanceExample(), which we use when we want to know how long something takes to run. Note that all test methods in XCTest need to start with the word "test". We get all this without having to write any code.

While we're here, let's add an assertion to the testExample() method. Change the testExample to the code in Listing 2-6 so you can see how the tests run in Xcode.

Listing 2-6. XCTAssert Unit Test

```
func testExample() {
    let result = 2+2
    XCTAssert(result == 4, "something gone wrong here")
}
```

Listing 2-6 tests that 2+2 is indeed equal to 4 using XCTAssert. The error string after the test is typically used to give you a hint about what test failed. But in this example, it's just a simple "something gone wrong here" catch-all error message.

Click on the test tab ◇ in the Navigator area so you can see the Test Navigator. Run the test by right-clicking on testExample() in the Test Navigator and choosing Test "testExample()". The green arrow indicates that it's a passing test. You should see the same view as shown in Figure 2-7.

Figure 2-7. *testExample test passes*

We can also see a report on how the tests ran if we right-click again on
testExample() in the Test Navigator and choose Jump to report. See Figure 2-8.

Figure 2-8. *Test report*

While we don't have that much to report yet, it does show us where we need to go
when we start writing more comprehensive unit tests.

To complete this app, you need to take the following steps:

1. Create the user interface or view.

2. Create the model code to perform the calculations.

Once that's completed, you can return to unit tests.

Creating the View

Figure 2-9 shows the calculator layout in `Main.Storyboard`. The numbers and the operations are buttons and we're using a text field to display the results.

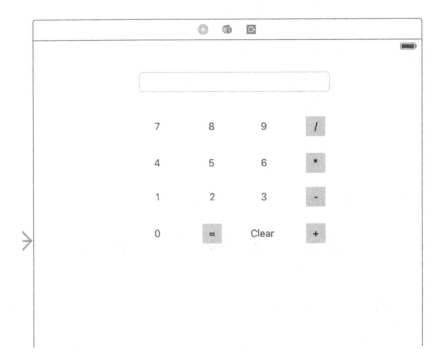

Figure 2-9. *Calculator layout*

Setting Up the User Interface

1. Click on `Main.Storyboard` in the Project Navigator.

2. Search for Text Field in the Object Library ⊙ at the bottom of the Utilities area.

3. Drag a Text Field onto the View Controller.

4. Click on the Size Inspector tab 📱 at the top of the Utilities area.

5. Set the measurements as follows:

    - X: 70

    - Y: 30

    - Width: 250

6. Going back to the Object Library, search for a Button.

7. Drag a Button and place it just under the left side of the text field.

8. Double-click on the Button and rename it the number 7.

9. Drag and rename the remaining buttons so that the View Controller looks like Figure 2-10.

Figure 2-10. *Calculator buttons and results text field*

Setting Up the Outlets

To connect the elements on the View Controller to the code, you need to first set up the outlets:

1. We want to make some room to show the `ViewController` `swift` code, so first click on 🗆 to hide the Document Outline.

2. Next click on Show the Assistant Window ⊘ to see the ViewController code.

3. Click on the number 7 at the same time as `control` and then drag it across to the code.

4. In the menu that pops up, choose the following and click Connect; see Figure 2-11.

    i.   Connection: Action

    ii. Name: compute

    iii. Type: UIButton

    iv. Event: Touch Up Inside

    v. Arguments: Sender

5. Repeat these steps for the remaining numbers.

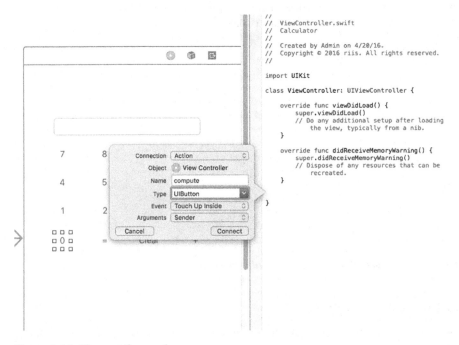

Figure 2-11. *Connect the numbers*

6. Hold control and drag the + field to the ViewController code.

7. In the menu that pops up, choose the following and click Connect; see Figure 2-12.

- Connection: Action
- Name: operation
- Type: UIButton
- Event: Touch Up Inside
- Arguments: Sender

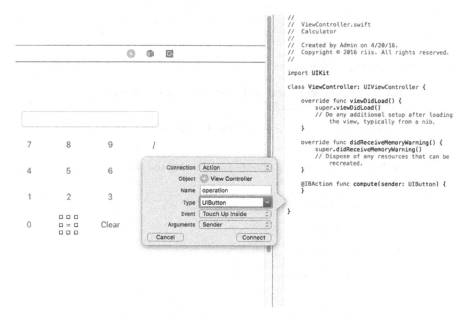

Figure 2-12. *Connect the operations*

8. Repeat this process for =, -, *, and /.

9. Next, hold Control and drag the Clear button to the code.

10. In the menu that pops up, choose the following and click Connect; see Figure 2-12.

- Connection: Action
- Name: clear
- Type: UIButton
- Event: Touch Up Inside
- Arguments: Sender

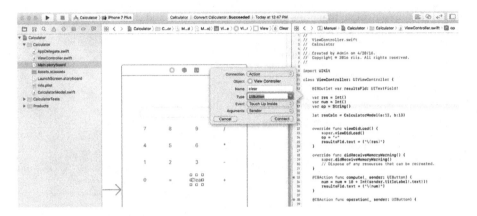

Figure 2-13. Connect the Clear button

11. Finally, we connect the text field where we are going to place the results of our calculations.

12. Hold control and drag the text field to the ViewController code.

13. In the menu that pops up, choose the following and click Connect; see Figure 2-14.

   • Connection: Outlet

   • Name: resultsFld

   • Type: UITextField

   • Storage: Strong

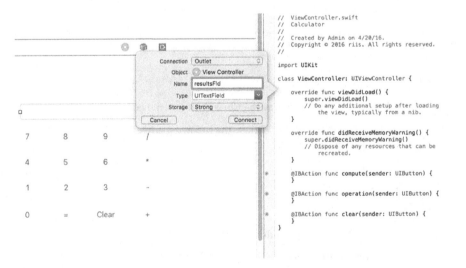

Figure 2-14. Connecting the Clear button

Completing the ViewController Code

Listing 2-7 shows the complete code for our ViewController, including the compute, operation, and clear fields. The operation code calls our `CalculatorModel` code, which performs the calculations. We need to isolate the operations or model code by putting it in a different class, which then makes it possible to unit test our code.

Listing 2-7. ViewController Code

```
import UIKit

class ViewController: UIViewController {
    @IBOutlet var resultsFld: UITextField!

    var res = Int()
    var num = Int()
    var op = String()

    let resCalc = CalculatorModel()

    override func viewDidLoad() {
        super.viewDidLoad()
        op = "="
        resultsFld.text = ("\(res)")
    }

    override func didReceiveMemoryWarning() {
        super.didReceiveMemoryWarning()
    }

    @IBAction func compute(sender: UIButton) {
        num = num * 10 + Int(sender.titleLabel!.text!)!
        resultsFld.text = ("\(num)")
    }

@IBAction func operation(sender: UIButton) {

    switch op {
        case "=":
            res = num
        case "+":
            res = resCalc.add(res, num)
        case "-":
            res = resCalc.sub(res, num)
        case "*":
            res = resCalc.mul(res, num)
        case "/":
            res = resCalc.div(res, num)
```

```
            default:
                print("error")
        }

        num = 0
        resultsFld.text = ("\(res)")

        if(sender.titleLabel!.text == "=") {
            res = 0
        }

        op = sender.titleLabel!.text! as String!

    }

    @IBAction func clear(sender: UIButton) {
        res = 0
        num = 0
        op = "="
        resultsFld.text = ("\(res)")
    }
}
```

Create the Model Code

The code for our Calculator model is shown in Listing 2-8. We have very simple add, sub, mul, and div functions. Note also that we're putting a guard around the div operation to protect against dividing by zero.

Listing 2-8. CalculatorModel.swift

```
import Foundation

class CalculatorModel {

    var a: Int!
    var b: Int!

    func add(_ a:Int,_ b:Int) -> Int {
        return a + b
    }

    func sub(_ a:Int,_ b:Int) -> Int {
        return a - b
    }
```

```swift
func mul(_ a:Int,_ b:Int) -> Int {
    return a * b
}

func div(_ a:Int,_ b:Int) -> Int {

    guard b != 0 else {
        return 0
    }
    return a / b
}

}
```

Tests

We now go back to `CalculatorTests.swift` in the `CalculatorTests` directory and add the `testAdd()` code in Listing 2-9. This file allows us to do some simple unit tests on the add method in the `CalculatorModel` class.

Listing 2-9. testAdd()

```swift
import XCTest
@testable import Calculator

class CalculatorTests: XCTestCase {

    var resCalc : CalculatorModel!

    override func setUp() {
      super.setUp()
      resCalc = CalculatorModel()
    }

    func testAdd() {
        XCTAssertEqual(resCalc.add(1, 1),2)
        XCTAssertEqual(resCalc.add(1, 2),3)
        XCTAssertEqual(resCalc.add(5, 4),9)
    }
}
```

Figure 2-15 shows the test results for our unit test in the Test Navigator. We also included a divide by zero test to make sure the guard is working effectively.

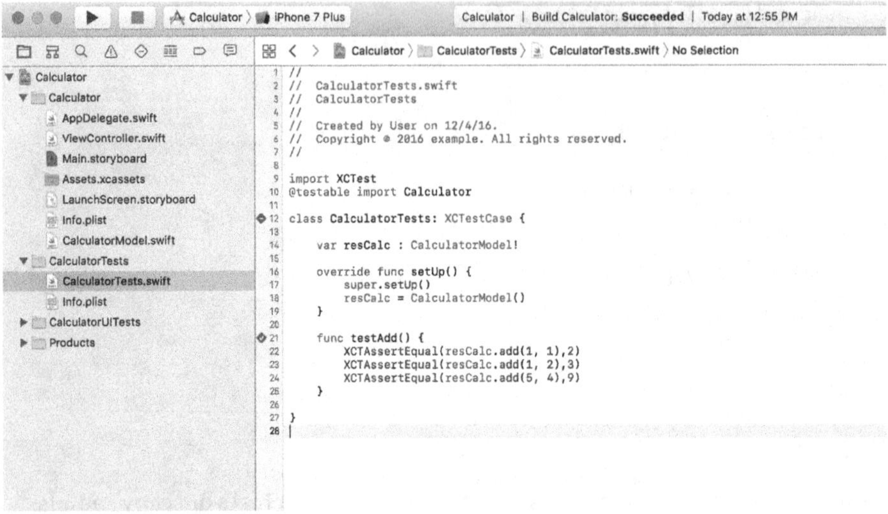

Figure 2-15. *Test results*

We can do a lot more with our Swift unit tests, which we'll talk about later in this chapter. But it is worth noting that it is simplicity itself to set up and use unit testing with the XCTest library for Swift in Xcode.

Unit Testing 102

We touched earlier on what makes a good unit test. At its most basic, a unit test should have the following "first" qualities, which were first coined by Tim Ottinger and Brett Schuchert:

- Fast
- Isolated
- Repeatable
- Self-verifying
- Timely

FIRST Unit Tests

There's no point in writing unit tests unless they finish *fast*. If they're too slow then over time they will get skipped as people get bored.

Unit tests should be *isolated* so that your tests don't have to worry about whether a third-party server is running or not or if the WiFi is down. We'll talk about how to do that in the chapter on mocking.

Unit tests should be *repeatable* and give you the same result each time. Users will lose confidence if your tests start to produce random behavior.

Unit tests should be *self-verifying*. We're familiar with the concept of assertions and we know that they are part of the Setup-Record-Verify process of unit testing. But are we sure that our unit tests are testing our code adequately? Are they only testing happy paths or are they also testing enough edge cases so we can be confident when we add new features? Code coverage can help us here and we'll talk about that later in this section.

Finally, unit tests should be *timely*, which means tests should not be written when all the code is completed to make your code coverage numbers look better. Write your unit tests as you write your code, preferably using Test Driven Development (TDD), which we cover in a later chapter. Best practices dictate that you need to understand the application code when you're writing your unit tests; otherwise, you're not going to know what to test and you're not going to write good tests.

Maintaining Your Unit Tests

So far we've only written a couple of tests, but what happens when you have 100s or 1000s of tests? Just like application code, unit tests can become unmaintainable and break easily as their numbers grow. We need to make sure that we're paying attention to the tests and practice refactoring them early and often.

We also need to make sure our unit tests have clear and concise error messages so we have some hope of finding out what error failed and why.

Error Messages

Like with application code, we quickly forget all the details of how the tests function. If we haven't written any tests in a while, it gets a lot more difficult to understand what was being tested and why. Writing optional error messages is one simple way to help reverse the process and give yourself hints that will hopefully jog your memory to remind you what you were testing.

XCTest assertions take two or more arguments, as you've seen in earlier examples. After the arguments comes the optional error message string; see Listing 2-10. XCTest will display the error message if the assertions fails. You can also include variable names in the error message to make the error message more meaningful.

Listing 2-10. Meaningful Error Messages

```
func testAdd() {
    XCTAssertEqual(resCalc.add(1,1),2,"testAdd failed - 1 + 1 does not equal
    2")
}
```

Xcode also allows you to filter on failed tests only, as shown in Figure 2-16, which can be useful as your tests start to grow exponentially.

Figure 2-16. *Filter to only show the failed tests*

Parameterized

Listing 2-11, shows a simple function that multiplies two inputs, a and b.

Listing 2-11. Multiply Function

```
func multiply(_ a: Int, _ b: Int) -> Int {
    return a * b
}
```

Instead of writing multiple lines of assert statements, we can use Swift parameters to write one XCTAssertEqual and pass in multiple tests, as shown in Listing 2-12. This makes for neater and more understandable tests.

Listing 2-12. Parameterized Tests

```
class MyTest: XCTestCase {

    func testMulParams() {
        let cases = [(4,3,12), (2,4,8), (3,5,15), (4,6,24)]
        cases.forEach {
            XCTAssertEqual(otherCalc.mul($0, $1), $2)
        }
    }

}
```

Code Coverage

Good code coverage is also essential to your unit testing. If the majority of your code is not covered by unit tests then you the risk of releasing untested code with defects.

To enable Code Coverage in your Swift app, go to Product ➤ Scheme ➤ Edit Scheme and check the Gather Coverage Data Code Coverage, as shown in Figure 2-17.

Figure 2-17. *Enable Code Coverage*

Xcode will show you what percentage of the code is covered by our tests. First choose the reporting tab (see Figure 2-18) and then click on the test results you want to look at (see the arrow in Figure 2-18). Then click on the Coverage tab.

Figure 2-18. *Code coverage*

Xcode also lets you see exactly what code is covered so you can immediately see the code that is covered by tests and perhaps more importantly what code is not covered. To see the code, click on the arrow beside the Swift file. In Figure 2-18, we're showing the arrow for CalculatorModel.swift.

Once you click on the code, you can see the code covered by tests in green and code that is not covered in red. See Figure 2-19.

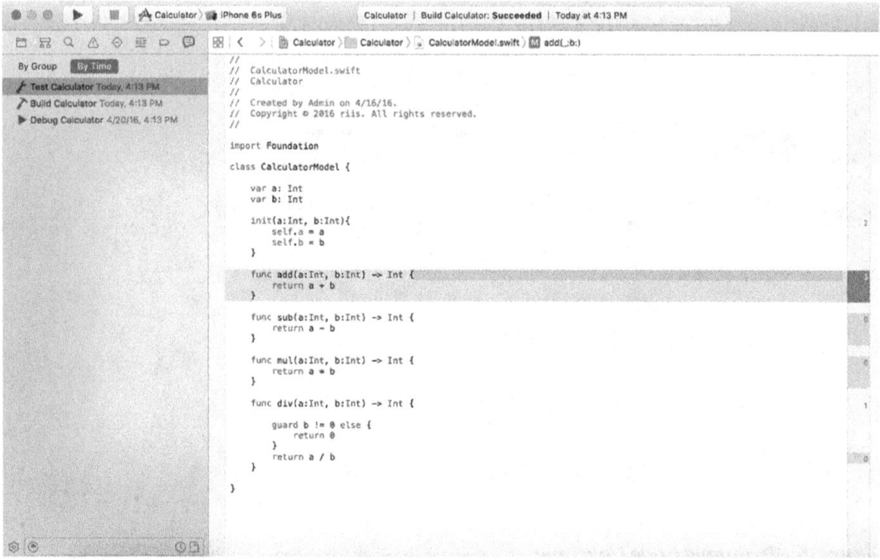

Figure 2-19. *Code covered by tests shown in green*

If we know where the untested code is, we need to fix it and make it green. We do this by writing more tests. Sometimes lots more tests so that all the red turns green. This in turn will increase our code coverage percentages.

When Things Go Wrong

Put it down to human nature, but you can be sure that there will be errors in your code and there will be errors in your tests. We talked earlier about how we can use optional error messages when a test fails, but what if the test is at fault and not your application code? Thankfully, you can set breakpoints in your test code to see what's happening.

In Figure 2-20, the test case XTAssertEqual(rescalc.add(1,2),3) has been changed to XTAssertEqual(rescalc.add(1,2),4) to make it fail. Figure 2-20 shows the failing test.

Figure 2-20. *Failing test*

Click on the offending line of code and then click on the blue breakpoint to set the breakpoint the next time the tests are run. Figure 2-21 shows Xcode when the breakpoint is encountered on a subsequent run.

Figure 2-21. *Debugging tests*

Xcode shows the value of each of the variables and you can either Step Into (F7) the called functions or Step Over (F6) code as appropriate. Changing the expected result back to 3 is enough to fix the error.

Figure 2-22 shows the Breakpoint tab, which lists all the breakpoints in the test or application code, which can be useful when you have multiple breakpoints set in your code.

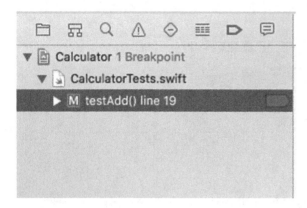

Figure 2-22. *Breakpoint tab*

Logs

If you run into any issues, one of the first places to look is the logs. You can find the logs in the Reporting tab, beside the Coverage tab in Xcode (see Figure 2-23). The logs will show the order that the tests are run in, as well as timings.

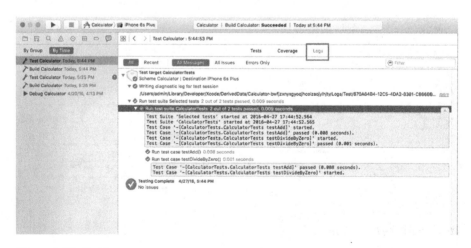

Figure 2-23. *Test logs*

If a test does fail, then the logs can be filtered to show errors only, as shown in Figure 2-24. In this example we've removed the guard condition from the divide function and caused an error by testing to see what happens when we divide by zero.

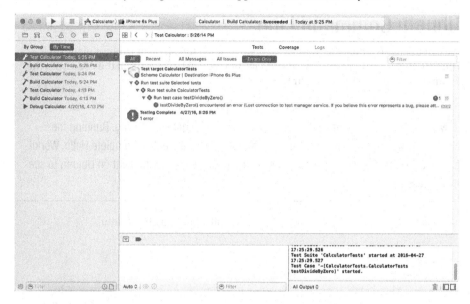

Figure 2-24. *Test error logs*

Clicking on the error will take you to errant code, as shown in Figure 2-25.

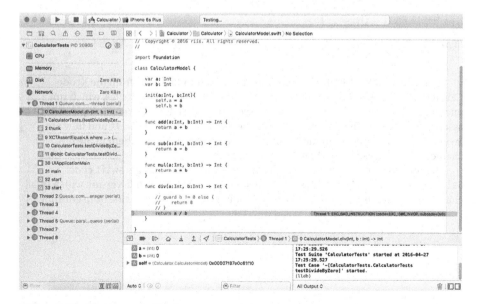

Figure 2-25. *Code error in Xcode*

We can fix the error by removing the comments so the guard can again catch the error before it crashes the program.

Ubuntu Command Line

We can build the model part of the Calculator app on the Linux or Ubuntu platform. Unfortunately, it won't have a user interface but we will be able to call the code from the command line as well as from our test suite.

■ **Note**   The structure of Swift apps on Ubuntu can be quite confusing. Running the command `swift package init` on the command line will create a complete Hello, World! example. This can be really useful when you're getting started with Swift on Ubuntu to see the correct structure of Swift app.

Figure 2-26 shows the tree structure of the Calculator app in Ubuntu.

```
├── Package.swift
├── Sources
│   └── Calculator.swift
└── Tests
    ├── Calculator
    │   ├── OtherCalculatorTests.swift
    │   └── SimpleCalculatorTests.swift
    └── LinuxMain.swift
```

Figure 2-26. *Calculator code*

Calculator.swift in the sources directory is our model code from the Xcode Calculator app. In the Tests/Calculator directory, we have two test files, which run a number of simple XCTAssertEquals and a second file that does the remaining available assertions. The two other files are Package.swift and LinuxMain.swift and they are Swift files that are needed on the Ubuntu platform. We touched on them in the last chapter and we'll also cover them later in this chapter.

To build the code, we need the Calculator code and the Package.swift code. Calculator.swift is shown in Listing 2-13. It's the same as the Xcode version with a small change, whereby we return 9999 when we divide by zero to stop the code from crashing.

Listing 2-13. Calculator.swift

```swift
class Calculator {

    func add(_ a:Int, _ b:Int) -> Int {
        return a + b
    }

    func sub(_ a:Int, _ b:Int) -> Int {
        return a - b
    }

    func mul(_ a:Int, _ b:Int) -> Int {
        return a * b
    }

    func div(_ a:Int, _ b:Int) -> Int {
        //divide by zero
        if (b == 0) {
            return 9999
        }
        return a / b
    }
}
```

Package.swift is our manifest file. It controls what code gets used in the build and what targets (debug, release) are going to get built. Our example is very simple; it just names the package, as shown in Listing 2-14.

Listing 2-14. Package Manager Code

```swift
import PackageDescription

let package = Package(
    name: "Calculator"
)
```

To build the files, type swift build.

If all goes well, you'll see a .build directory, with contents similar to that shown in Figure 2-27.

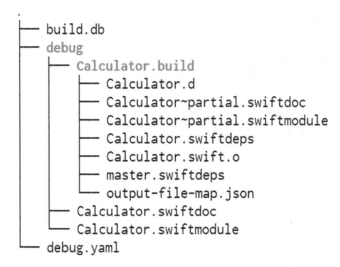

```
├── build.db
├── debug
│   ├── Calculator.build
│   │   ├── Calculator.d
│   │   ├── Calculator~partial.swiftdoc
│   │   ├── Calculator~partial.swiftmodule
│   │   ├── Calculator.swiftdeps
│   │   ├── Calculator.swift.o
│   │   ├── master.swiftdeps
│   │   └── output-file-map.json
│   ├── Calculator.swiftdoc
│   └── Calculator.swiftmodule
└── debug.yaml
```

Figure 2-27. *The build directory*

The build directory shows that we built the debug version of the app. There's not a lot of information here that's immediately useful, although we can see the modules external dependencies—Calculator.swiftdefs—as well as what compiles and flags were used to compile the module—debug.yaml—which is useful when trying to find the root of a problem.

To run the Calculator code, we create a new main.swift file in the sources directory, as shown in Listing 2-15.

Listing 2-15. main.swift

```
let foobar = Calculator()
var result = foobar.add(1,2)
print("Total: \(result)")
```

Rebuild the code again using the Swift build command and then run the executable by calling .build/debug/Calculator. This gives the following result:

```
$ .build/debug/Calculator
Total: 3
```

Package Manager

Package managers can be a lot more complex than our example, which has only a name value. We can also include other source code dependencies and include or exclude directories from the build process. Listing 2-16, shows a Package.swift example called DeckOfPlayingCards that comes from Swift.org. In the file, it includes a couple of other repositories that are included when the module is built.

Listing 2-16. Package.swift File from DeckOfPlayingCards

```swift
import PackageDescription

let package = Package(
    name: "DeckOfPlayingCards",
    dependencies: [
        .Package(url: "https://github.com/apple/example-package-fisheryates.
          git", majorVersion: 1),
        .Package(url: "https://github.com/apple/example-package-playingcard.
          git", majorVersion: 1),
    ]
)
```

Tests

For our calculator example, we have two files for simple and edge case tests, SimpleCalculatorTests and OtherCalculatorTests. Figure 2-28 shows how the Tests directory is structured.

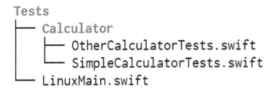

Figure 2-28. *Test code directory structure*

The test methods in SimpleCalculatorTests—testAddTwoNumbersCheck, testSubTwoNumbersCheck, testMulTwoNumbersCheck, and testDivTwoNumbersCheck— test the straightforward operation of the calculator. The test methods in the OtherCalculatorTests—testSubWorksWithNegativeResult, testMulByZeroCheck, testMulNotEqual, testMulLessThan, testMulGreaterThan, testMulParams, and testDivByZeroCheck—show examples of some other XCTAsserts, as well as use a parameterized test for neater tests and a test to see what happens when you divide by zero.

Any of the tests we create for the Ubuntu platform will also run within Xcode. But the opposite isn't always true. Most notably, performance tests do not work on the Ubuntu platform in Swift 3.

In both platforms the unit test methods are the same, so we import XCTest and use the @testable keyword to import the modules we want to test against. However, there are differences. XCTest needs to know the name of all the test methods in your code.

In both our test files we have an allTests extension with the name of the file SimpleCalculatorTests and a list of all the tests in the format shown in Listing 2-17. If you do not include a test method in allTests, it will not get called.

Listing 2-17. allTests Extension

```
extension SimpleCalculatorTests {
    static var allTests : [(String, (SimpleCalculatorTests) -> () throws ->
    Void)] {
        return [
            ("testAddTwoNumbersCheck", testAddTwoNumbersCheck),
            ("testSubTwoNumbersCheck", testSubTwoNumbersCheck),
            ("testMulTwoNumbersCheck", testMulTwoNumbersCheck),
            ("testDivTwoNumbersCheck", testDivTwoNumbersCheck)
        ]
    }
}
```

Finally, we need a LinuxMain.swift file that sets up the allTests variables for swift-test, as shown in Listing 2-18. The format is the same; you just change the names of the test suite and test case to match whatever you want to call your test suite.

Listing 2-18. LinuxMain.swift

```
import XCTest
@testable import CalculatorTests

XCTMain([
    testCase(CalculatorTests.allTests)
])
```

Simple Tests

Listing 2-19 shows the complete code for SimpleCalculatorTests.swift. It has the allTests extensions, a setUp and tearDown method, and the four tests to add, multiply, subtract, and divide a pair of numbers.

Listing 2-19. Simple Tests

```
import XCTest
@testable import Calculator

extension SimpleCalculatorTests {
    static var allTests : [(String, (SimpleCalculatorTests) -> () throws ->
    Void)] {
        return [
            ("testAddTwoNumbersCheck", testAddTwoNumbersCheck),
            ("testSubTwoNumbersCheck", testSubTwoNumbersCheck),
            ("testMulTwoNumbersCheck", testMulTwoNumbersCheck),
            ("testDivTwoNumbersCheck", testDivTwoNumbersCheck)
        ]
    }
}
```

```swift
class SimpleCalculatorTests: XCTestCase {

  var simpleCalc : Calculator!

  override func setUp() {
    super.setUp()
    simpleCalc = Calculator()
  }

  override func tearDown() {
    simpleCalc = nil
  }

  func testAddTwoNumbersCheck() {
    XCTAssertEqual(simpleCalc.add(1,1),2)
  }

  func testSubTwoNumbersCheck() {
    XCTAssertEqual(simpleCalc.sub(3,1),2)
  }

  func testMulTwoNumbersCheck() {
    XCTAssertEqual(simpleCalc.mul(2,3),6)
  }

  func testDivTwoNumbersCheck() {
    XCTAssertEqual(simpleCalc.div(12,2),6)
  }

}
```

Edge Case Tests

So far we've only used XCTAssertEqual. In our simplified view of the world, we only tested the happy path where things don't go wrong. But there are many scenarios that your code may encounter that are not so happy, such as dividing by zero. You have to make sure that the code will handle these unexpected scenarios. These examples show a few negative test examples as well as a few other miscellaneous tests.

In OtherCalculatorTests.swift, we have examples of XCTAssertNotEqual, XCTAssertLessThan, XCTAssertGreaterThan, a parameterized test shown earlier in the chapter, and also a test to make sure the calculator doesn't crash when we divide by zero. See Listing 2-20.

Listing 2-20. Edge Case Tests

```swift
import XCTest
@testable import Calculator
```

```swift
extension OtherCalculatorTests {
    static var allTests : [(String, (OtherCalculatorTests) -> () throws ->
    Void)] {
        return [
            ("testSubWorksWithNegativeResult",
            testSubWorksWithNegativeResult),
            ("testMulByZeroCheck", testMulByZeroCheck),
            ("testMulNotEqual", testMulNotEqual),
            ("testMulLessThan", testMulLessThan),
            ("testMulGreaterThan", testMulGreaterThan),
            ("testMulParams", testMulParams),
            ("testDivByZeroCheck", testDivByZeroCheck)
        ]
    }
}

class OtherCalculatorTests: XCTestCase {

  var otherCalc : Calculator!

  override func setUp() {
    super.setUp()
    otherCalc = Calculator()
  }

  override func tearDown() {
    otherCalc = nil
  }

  func testSubWorksWithNegativeResult() {
    XCTAssertEqual(otherCalc.sub(1,3),-2)
  }

  func testMulByZeroCheck() {
    XCTAssertEqual(otherCalc.mul(2,0),0)
  }

  func testMulNotEqual() {
    XCTAssertNotEqual(otherCalc.mul(2,2),5)
  }

  func testMulLessThan() {
    XCTAssertLessThan(otherCalc.mul(2,2),5)
  }

  func testMulGreaterThan() {
    XCTAssertGreaterThan(otherCalc.mul(2,3),5)
  }
```

```
func testMulParams() {
    let cases = [(4,3,12), (2,4,8), (3,5,15), (4,6,24)]
    cases.forEach {
        XCTAssertEqual(otherCalc.mul($0, $1), $2)
    }
}

func testDivByZeroCheck() {
    XCTAssertEqual(otherCalc.div(12,0),9999)
}

}
```

Test Output

Even though there is more than one test file, we can run all the tests using the `swift test` command.

■ **Note**   Remove the `main.swift` class in the `sources` directory and rebuild using `swift build` before you run any tests.

```
$ swift test
Compile Swift Module 'CalculatorTests' (2 sources)
Linking ./.build/debug/CalculatorPackageTests.xctest
Test Suite 'All tests' started at 18:38:59.671
Test Suite 'debug.xctest' started at 18:38:59.680
Test Suite 'SimpleCalculatorTests' started at 18:38:59.680
Test Case 'SimpleCalculatorTests.testAddTwoNumbersCheck' started at
18:38:59.680
Test Case 'SimpleCalculatorTests.testAddTwoNumbersCheck' passed (0.0
seconds).
Test Case 'SimpleCalculatorTests.testSubTwoNumbersCheck' started at
18:38:59.680
Test Case 'SimpleCalculatorTests.testSubTwoNumbersCheck' passed (0.0
seconds).
Test Case 'SimpleCalculatorTests.testMulTwoNumbersCheck' started at
18:38:59.680
Test Case 'SimpleCalculatorTests.testMulTwoNumbersCheck' passed (0.0
seconds).
Test Case 'SimpleCalculatorTests.testDivTwoNumbersCheck' started at
18:38:59.680
Test Case 'SimpleCalculatorTests.testDivTwoNumbersCheck' passed (0.0
seconds).
Test Suite 'SimpleCalculatorTests' passed at 18:38:59.681
```

```
         Executed 4 tests, with 0 failures (0 unexpected) in 0.0 (0.0) seconds
Test Suite 'OtherCalculatorTests' started at 18:38:59.681
Test Case 'OtherCalculatorTests.testSubWorksWithNegativeResult' started at
18:38:59.681
Test Case 'OtherCalculatorTests.testSubWorksWithNegativeResult' passed (0.0
seconds).
Test Case 'OtherCalculatorTests.testMulByZeroCheck' started at 18:38:59.681
Test Case 'OtherCalculatorTests.testMulByZeroCheck' passed (0.0 seconds).
Test Case 'OtherCalculatorTests.testMulNotEqual' started at 18:38:59.681
Test Case 'OtherCalculatorTests.testMulNotEqual' passed (0.0 seconds).
Test Case 'OtherCalculatorTests.testMulLessThan' started at 18:38:59.681
Test Case 'OtherCalculatorTests.testMulLessThan' passed (0.0 seconds).
Test Case 'OtherCalculatorTests.testMulGreaterThan' started at 18:38:59.681
Test Case 'OtherCalculatorTests.testMulGreaterThan' passed (0.0 seconds).
Test Case 'OtherCalculatorTests.testMulParams' started at 18:38:59.681
Test Case 'OtherCalculatorTests.testMulParams' passed (0.0 seconds).
Test Case 'OtherCalculatorTests.testDivByZeroCheck' started at 18:38:59.681
Test Case 'OtherCalculatorTests.testDivByZeroCheck' passed (0.0 seconds).
Test Suite 'OtherCalculatorTests' passed at 18:38:59.681
         Executed 7 tests, with 0 failures (0 unexpected) in 0.0 (0.0) seconds
Test Suite 'debug.xctest' passed at 18:38:59.681
 Executed 11 tests, with 0 failures (0 unexpected) in 0.0 (0.0) seconds
Test Suite 'All tests' passed at 18:38:59.681
         Executed 11 tests, with 0 failures (0 unexpected) in 0.0 (0.0) seconds
```

Summary

In this chapter, we looked at XCTest in more detail. It's not as comprehensive as OCUnit, but for what you lose in functionality, it's more than made up by XCTest's simplicity. And, no doubt, there will be changes coming in future versions of Swift.

Before we leave, it's worth pointing out that unit testing requires time. The toy examples in this chapter rapidly expand along with your code. Development takes longer as you're writing more tests, but QA time should be reduced—especially any manual testing. If you have good coverage it will extend the life of your code considerably, as you don't have to fight spaghetti code to add just one more slice of functionality.

But we'd be lying if we said that unit testing on its own is the holy grail. There are many more elements to creating Agile Swift code. We haven't mentioned mocks, where Swift has some interesting limitations. We'll cover that in Chapter 4. We have only briefly touched on UI testing; we'll cover that in more detail in Chapter 5. And we'll also return to unit testing and more specifically to Test Driven Development in Chapter 6.

In the next chapter, we'll look at which tools from Apple and others can help us create cleaner, faster, and neater unit tests.

CHAPTER 3

■ ■ ■

Third-Party Tools

You are going to need some extra third-party tools to make sure your tests are FIRST class tests. Or, in other words, that they are:

- Fast

- Isolated

- Repeatable

- Self-verifying

- Timely

XCTest isn't going to be enough to satisfy the first criteria. If we were using Objective-C this is pretty straightforward. In Objective-C, we use OCUnit for our unit tests (fast) and OCMock (isolated) to mock out our interactions with anything outside the class we are testing. We also use Jenkins or our favorite continuous integration server (repeatable) to make the tests and gcovr for code coverage (self-verifying). And finally, we write the tests using a TDD approach (timely).

It's more complicated in Swift, but the FIRST principles are still the same. We want to make our unit tests as fast and expressive as possible. Because of the underlying design of the Swift language we don't have an XCMock and probably never will—but there are alternatives that we can use to isolate our code. We can do continuous integration and display our code coverage. And we can practice TDD in any language.

In this chapter, we'll look at what Xcode and third-party tool options are currently available and how you can use them to write better tests.

Note that many of these third-party tools continue to experience significant changes as Swift evolves. Some of them will fade away and others will take their place. Check the source code at http://github.com/godfreynolan/agileswift to find the latest working examples.

Fast Tests

XCTest does help you in the fast category of the FIRST criteria. But it many cases it may not be expressive enough for what you want to test. Nimble, on the other hand, will provide you with the testing power you need to test your code quickly and help to make sure you're testing the right thing.

Anything more than a simple Hello, World type application is probably going to need better assertions than what comes with the XCTest assertions. Nimble is one option that offers a lot more matchers. It also provides a lot more flexibility by allowing you to include ranges instead of just single values. Nimble lets you create matchers that can be combined to create much more flexible expressions of intent than XCTest.

Table 3-1 lists most of the Nimble assertions and you can also write your own. Note that each of these assertions also has the negative or NOT version of the assertion. This table does not include any custom matchers, which are also supported in Nimble.

■ **Note**   Nimble goes hand in hand with Quick, which is a BDD or Behavior Driven Design Framework we'll cover more about UI testing in Chapter 5.

Nimble Install

The easiest way to install Nimble is to use CocoaPods, which is another dependency manager for iOS and Cocoa projects. Before we can install Nimble, we have to install CocoaPods, which we do as follows.

```
sudo gem install cocoapods
pod setup --verbose
```

Now we can install Nimble. cd to the project directory and type the command

```
pod init
```

This creates a podfile. If we're using this on the Calculator code, then edit the podfile so it looks like Listing 3-1.

Listing 3-1. Nimble Podfile

```
platform :ios, '9.0'
source 'https://github.com/CocoaPods/Specs.git'

target 'CalculatorTests' do
        use_frameworks!
        pod 'Quick'
        pod 'Nimble', '~> 4.0.0'
end
```

Lastly we have to execute the podfile so it downloads and installs Nimble. Type the following to run the podfile.

```
pod install
```

Table 3-1. *Nimble Matchers*

Assertion Type	Description	Example
Equivalence	Passes if actual is equivalent to expected	`expect(actual).to(equal(expected))`
Identity	Passes if actual has the same pointer address as expected	`expect(actual).to(beIdenticalTo(expected))`
Comparison	`LessThan`, `LessThanOrEqualTo`, `GreaterThan`, and `GreaterThanOrEqualTo`	`expect(actual).to(beLessThan(expected))`
Comparison	Passes if expected is close to actual within a tolerance	`expect(actual).to(beCloseTo(expected, within: delta))`
Types/Classes	Passes if instance is an instance of a class	`expect(instance).to(beAnInstanceOf(aClass))`
Truthiness	Passes if actual is not nil, true, or an object with a Boolean value of true	`expect(actual).to(beTruthy())`
Error Handling	Passes if `somethingThatThrows()` throws an `ErrorType`	`expect{ try somethingThatThrows() }.to(throwError())`
Collection Membership	Passes if all of the expected values are members of actual	`expect(["whale", "dolphin", "starfish"]).to(contain("dolphin", "starfish"))`
Strings	Passes if actual contains, beginsWith, endsWith, or empty substring expected	`expect(actual).to(contain(expected))`
Count	Passes if actual collection's count is equal to expected	`expect(actual).to(haveCount(expected))`
Group of Matchers	Matches a value to any of a group of matchers	`expect(actual).to(satisfyAnyOf (beLessThan(10), beGreaterThan(20)))`

Nimble Unit Test

To use Nimble in our tests, we need to import the Nimble library. We can then replace some of our earlier tests with expect statements, such as

```
expect(self.resCalc.add(1,operandTwo: 1)) == 2
```

Or we can create more complex matchers such as this range.

```
expect(self.resCalc.mul(4, operandTwo: 3)).to(satisfyAnyOf(beGreaterTh
an(10), beLessThan(20)))
```

The full code is shown in Listing 3-2.

Listing 3-2. Nimble Unit Tests

```
import XCTest
import Nimble
@testable import Calculator

class CalculatorTests: XCTestCase {

    let resCalc = CalculatorModel()

    func testAdd() {
        expect(self.resCalc.add(1,1)) == 2
    }

    func testAddRange() {
        expect(self.resCalc.mul(4, 3)).to(satisfyAnyOf(beGreaterThan(10),
        beLessThan(20)))
    }

}
```

Nimble integrated with XCTest is an excellent Swift matcher framework. CocoaPods also makes it easy to install and configure.

Isolated Unit Tests

In the last chapter, we talked about how unit tests should be isolated so that your tests don't have to worry about whether a third-party server is running or if the WiFi is down. Writing and executing unit tests should be lightning fast. To do this, we need to write method-based unit tests with mocked out database or network access.

If we're making network connections or reading from the file system or database, then by definition we're not writing isolated unit tests. We are also making an assumption about a third-party web service or database that may not be running every time we run our tests. In a worst-case scenario, our tests are going to fail, but for the wrong reason such as the network being down.

To keep our unit tests isolated from any outside interference, we need to mock out any code that talks to external resources.

Mocking

The classic way to isolate your code in most languages is to use a *mocking* framework. Mocking works by interrupting any calls that we want to isolate our tests from and replacing them with fake code that returns a known result. For example, say we want to test how our parser code works with a web service. We're going to assume that the web service knows what it's doing and passes our JSON parser code a known JSON string of objects. If we're testing our JSON parser code, we don't care about the web service, because that's the responsibility of some other test, probably an integration test. Mocking allows us to provide this type of isolated testing.

Similarly, what if we're trying to test our login authentication code? It's not our job to test if SQLite works correctly; we just want to test the decryption code. So we isolate SQLite by mocking out the calls and passing in a fake username and encrypted password into our methods being tested.

In Objective-C, the mocking framework would possibly be OCMock and in Java it would probably be Mockito or PowerMock. Unfortunately things aren't as simple in Swift because the Swift runtime won't allow these mocking frameworks to inject code to mock out the classes we want to isolate our code from. However, all is not lost. We can still mock out the calls but it's not as neat and tidy in Swift. It's still possible to isolate your tests from outside influences by stubbing out the methods or using one of the few emerging frameworks.

What Is Mocking

Mocking can be confusing, but it can be summarized by the following code:

```
when(methodIsCalled).thenReturn(aValue);
```

When `methodIsCalled`, it always returns `aValue`; for example, when you call `getWeatherForCity("Troy")` then always return 72 or if you call `getDateAndTime()` then always return `{"time": "12:43:12 PM","date": "05-30-2016"}`.

The concept is that the temperature or time is then used to test your target methods. You can always rely on it being what you hardcoded so you can spend time trying to break your Fahrenheit to Celsius conversion or your JSON parsers.

You can also mock edge cases, such as impossible temperatures (-460) or different time zones (GMT), to see how your code handles it.

There are three parts to creating this mocking behavior:

- *Arrange*: Set up the testing objects

- *Act*: Perform the actual test

- *Assert*: Verify the result

In Listing 3-3, we set up or arrange the test objects in the arrange phase, in this case a particular date. We act or test the object and verify that the date exists and is as expected.

Listing 3-3. Arrange, Act, and Assert

```
stub(mock) {
    (mock) in
    when(mock.getDate.get).thenReturn(dateAndTime.from(year: 2014, month:
    05, day: 20) as Date)
}
XCTAssertEqual(mock.getDate, dateAndTime.from(year: 2014, month: 05, day:
20) as Date)
XCTAssertNotNil(verify(mock).getDate)
```

In the example we're using a framework called Cuckoo, which is available from `https://github.com/SwiftKit/Cuckoo`. It gets around the read-only binary restrictions by using a two-stage process. The first stage generates the mocking code from your test objects, which is then recompiled in the second stage so you fake your object calls.

To install Cuckoo, take the following steps:

1. Create your project with model class and test class.

2. Install the Cuckoo pod by first running pod init from the command line.

3. Edit the generated podfile and add pod "Cuckoo" as a test target.

4. Run the command pod install.

5. Close the project and reopen the workspace.

6. Click on the project folder then choose Test Target ➤ Build Phases. See Figure 3-1.

7. Click + and choose New Run Script Phase.

8. Add Listing 3-4 to the Run Script section, making sure to modify the input files that you want to mock.

9. Build the project.

10. Run the tests.

11. Drag and drop GeneratedMocks.swift into the test section.

12. Run the mocked tests.

Listing 3-4. Cuckoo Run Script

```
# Define output file; change "${PROJECT_NAME}Tests" to your test's root
source folder, if it's not the default name
OUTPUT_FILE="./${PROJECT_NAME}Tests/GeneratedMocks.swift"
echo "Generated Mocks File = ${OUTPUT_FILE}"
```

```
# Define input directory; change "${PROJECT_NAME}" to your project's root
source folder, if it's not the default name
INPUT_DIR="./${PROJECT_NAME}"
echo "Mocks Input Directory = ${INPUT_DIR}"

# Generate mock files; include as many input files as you'd like to create
mocks for
${PODS_ROOT}/Cuckoo/run generate --testable "${PROJECT_NAME}" \
--output "${OUTPUT_FILE}" \
"${INPUT_DIR}/FileName1.swift" \
"${INPUT_DIR}/FileName2.swift" \
"${INPUT_DIR}/FileName3.swift"
# ... and so forth

# After running once, locate `GeneratedMocks.swift` and drag it into your
Xcode test target group
```

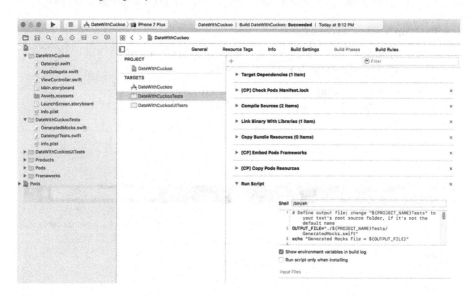

Figure 3-1. *Adding a run script*

In the next chapter, we'll take a more detailed look at how to mock web services, dates, and system properties in Swift using Cuckoo.

Repeatable Unit Tests

Continuous integration means that you should be building your app early and building it often. You should be building the code from the earliest stages of your development process and you should building on a regular basis—every evening or alternatively every time the code is checked in.

Because it's more of a DevOps process, it doesn't belong on a development machine. Ideally, it should be on a standalone machine, such as a Mac Pro Server, or in the cloud. That allows everyone to see the build reports and metrics.

We're going to use Jenkins as our continuous integration build server. You may be asking yourself why we wouldn't just use an OSX server as our build server. If you're working in an environment where you're only doing iOS development, then the OSX server is a good option, but if you're working in a mixed environment—even if it's a mixed Swift environment—then OSX server isn't going to work. Personally, I like to be able see how all the Java, PHP, Objective-C, and Swift builds are doing in the same place, so Jenkins is the best option.

Installing Jenkins

Sometimes tools are easy to set up and sometimes they are not. Unfortunately on a Mac, Jenkins falls into the latter category. Once you have it up and running for a single project then it's very easy to configure. But it can be surprisingly difficult to get the first project working.

To set up Jenkins, take the following steps:

1. Download the latest LTS (long-term support) version of Jenkins from `http://jenkins-ci.org`.

2. Install the package. When it's completed, go to `http://localhost:8080`, where you should see something like Figure 3-2.

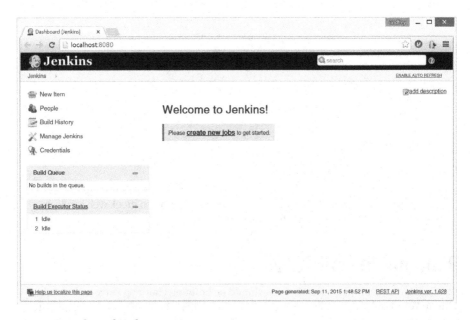

Figure 3-2. The Jenkins home page

To make it useful in our Swift environment, we need to add a number of plugins. Click on Manage Jenkins ➤ Manage Plugins and search for and add the Xcode and Git plugin or whatever other source code management system you use. When you're done, your installed plugins screen should look something like Figure 3-3.

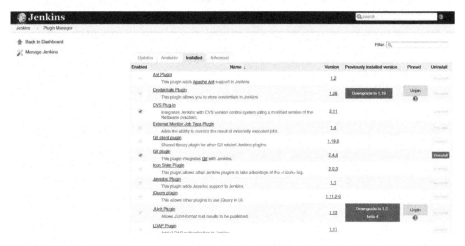

Figure 3-3. *Jenkins plugins*

We've already touched on why our Jenkins server should be a dedicated box. The hardest part of the configuration process is to set it up so it has the correct permissions to run the iOS simulator.

Take the following steps to give Jenkins the correct permissions:

1. Set up the user `jenkins` correctly as the install misses a couple of things, as shown in Figure 3-4.

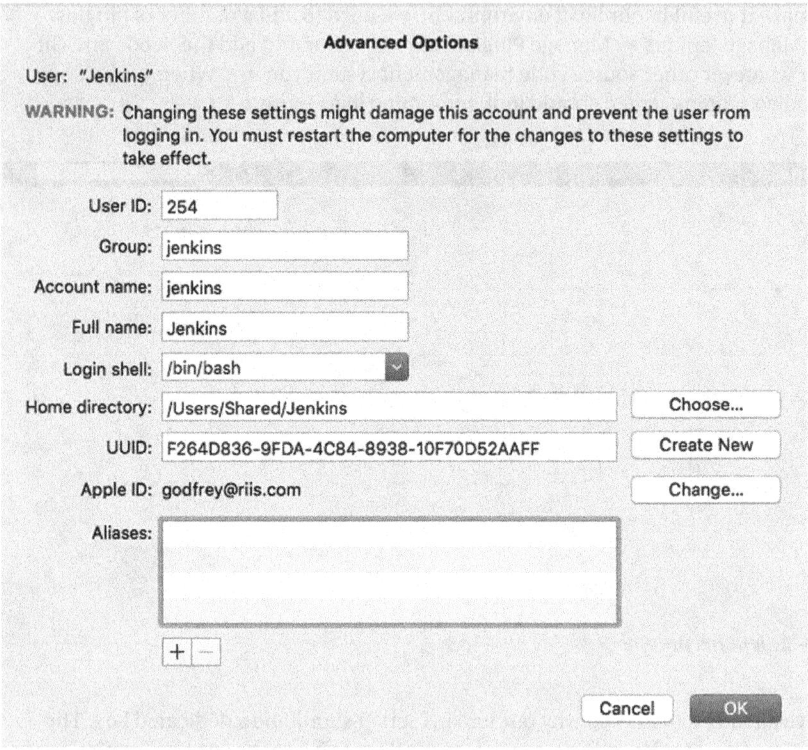

Figure 3-4. *Configure the Jenkins user*

2. Make jenkins an admin user as follows:

```
sudo dseditgroup -o edit -a jenkins -t user admin
```

3. Add jenkins to the developer group:

```
sudo dscl . append /Groups/_developer GroupMembership jenkins
```

4. Click on the Login options, set Autologin as Jenkins, and then reboot. See Figure 3-5.

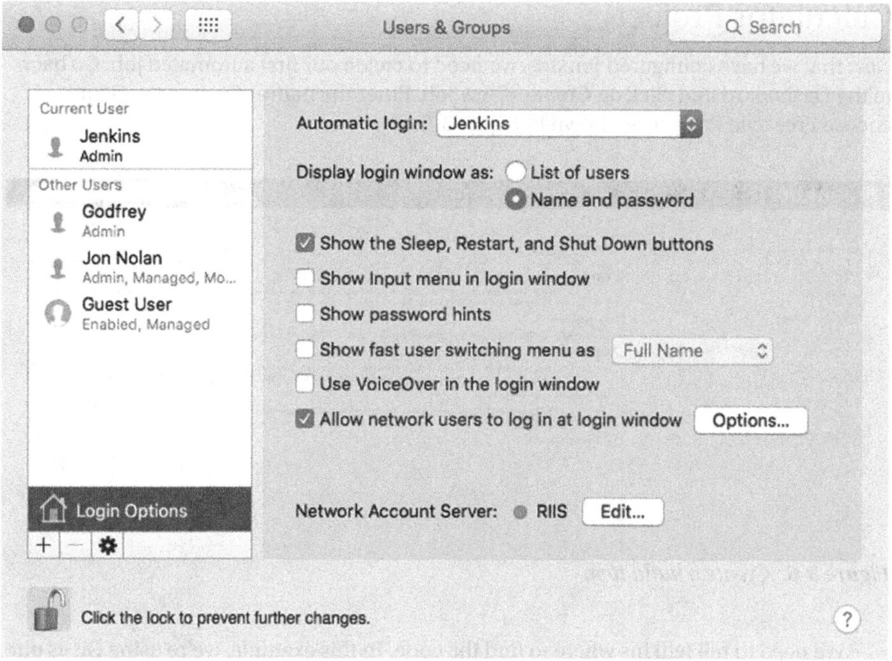

Figure 3-5. Autologin as a Jenkins user

5. Make the Jenkins application run as a launch agent and not as a daemon so the simulator can run correctly. We need to first unload the Jenkins app and then move it. Execute the following commands from the terminal.

```
sudo launchctl unload /Library/LaunchDaemons/org.jenkins-ci.plist
sudo mv /Library/LaunchDaemons/org.jenkins-ci.plist /Library/
LaunchAgents/
```

6. Remove the following lines from the org.jenkins-ci.plist file.

```
<key>SessionCreate</key>
<true />
```

7. Finally, reload the Jenkins app by executing the following commands in the terminal.

```
sudo launchctl load /Library/LaunchAgents/org.jenkins-ci.plist
sudo dseditgroup -o edit -a jenkins -t user admin
```

71

Calculator Project

Now that we have configured Jenkins, we need to create our first automated job. Go back to the Dashboard and click on Create a New Job. Enter the name of your project and choose Freestyle Project, as shown in Figure 3-6.

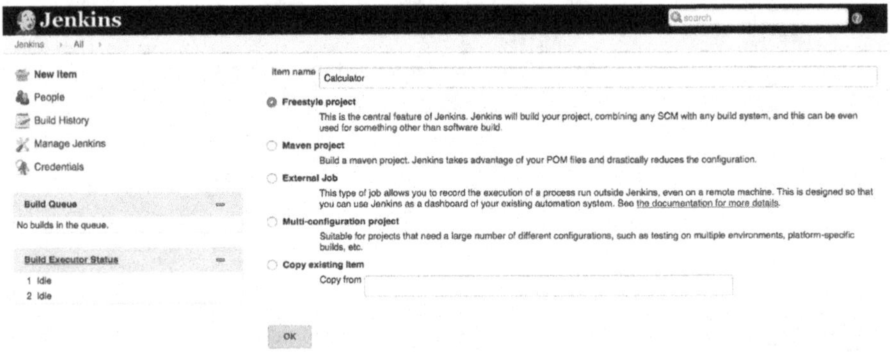

Figure 3-6. *Create a build Item*

We need to tell Jenkins where to find the code. In this example, we're using Git as our source code management system. Here we're again we're using the Calculator example. Enter the Git repository URL. As it's a public repo, there are no credentials so we're going to skip that. There is also only one branch so we can leave the Branch Specifier as the master. See Figure 3-7.

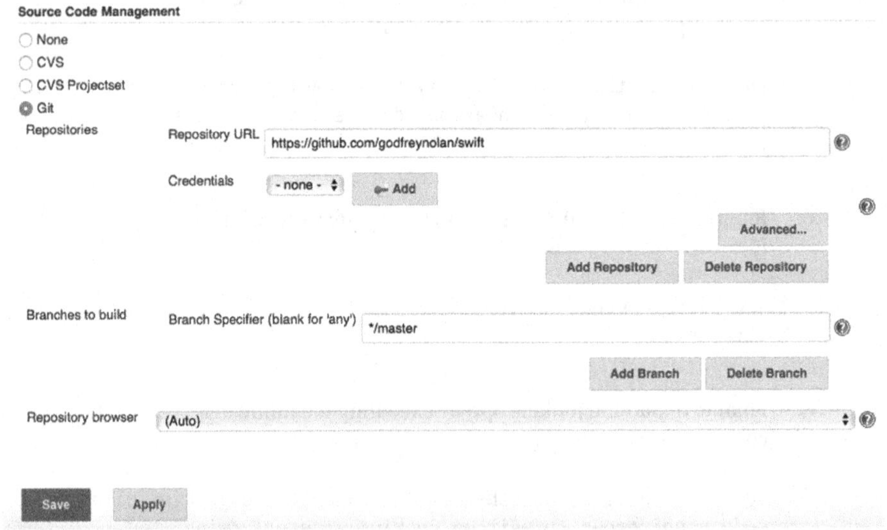

Figure 3-7. *Source code management*

Scroll down to the Build section and choose the Xcode build action. See Figure 3-8.

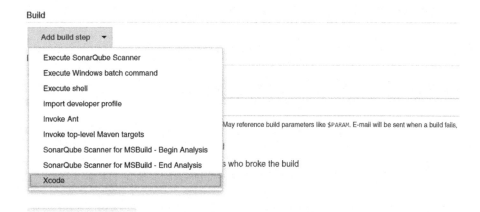

Figure 3-8. The Xcode build step

In the Xcode build step, click on Settings and change the configuration to Debug, as shown in Figure 3-9.

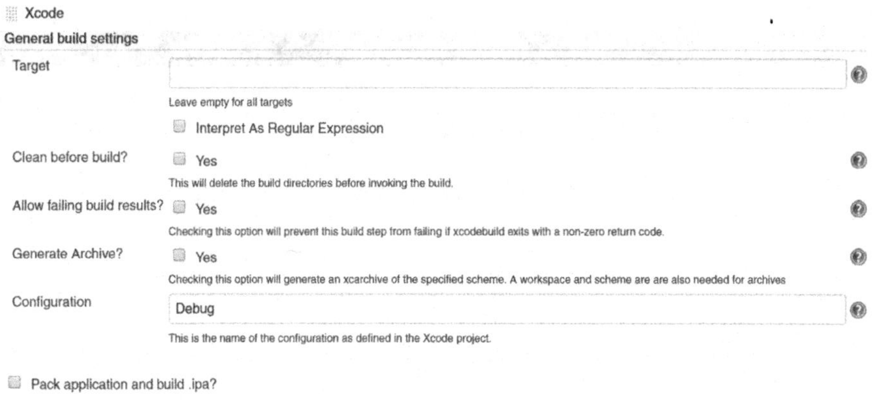

Figure 3-9. *Xcode settings*

Scroll down and click on Advanced Build Setting and set the Xcode Schema File to Calculator and the custom xcodebuild arguments to "test -destination 'platform=iOS Simulator,name=iPhone 6s Plus,OS=9.3'". This tells Xcode to run the tests using the iPhone 6s Plus simulator running iOS 9.3. See Figure 3-10. This may need to change for you depending on what you have installed on your machine. Click Save to save your configuration.

73

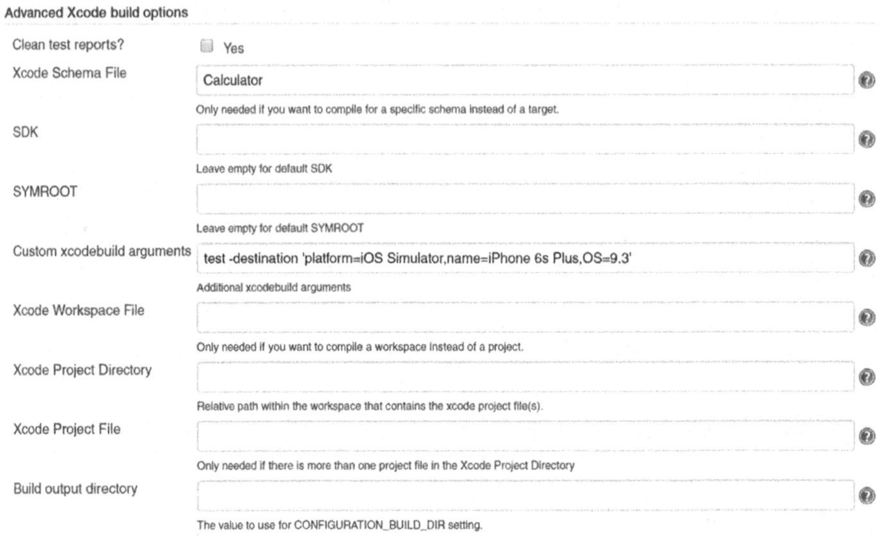
Advanced Xcode build options
Clean test reports?
Yes
Xcode Schema File
Calculator
Only needed if you want to compile for a specific schema instead of a target.
SDK
Leave empty for default SDK
SYMROOT
Leave empty for default SYMROOT
Custom xcodebuild arguments
test -destination 'platform=iOS Simulator,name=iPhone 6s Plus,OS=9.3'
Additional xcodebuild arguments
Xcode Workspace File
Only needed if you want to compile a workspace instead of a project.
Xcode Project Directory
Relative path within the workspace that contains the xcode project file(s).
Xcode Project File
Only needed if there is more than one project file in the Xcode Project Directory
Build output directory
The value to use for CONFIGURATION_BUILD_DIR setting.

Figure 3-10. *Advanced Xcode settings*

Now we're ready to build our app. Click on Build Now on the Project page. See Figure 3-11.

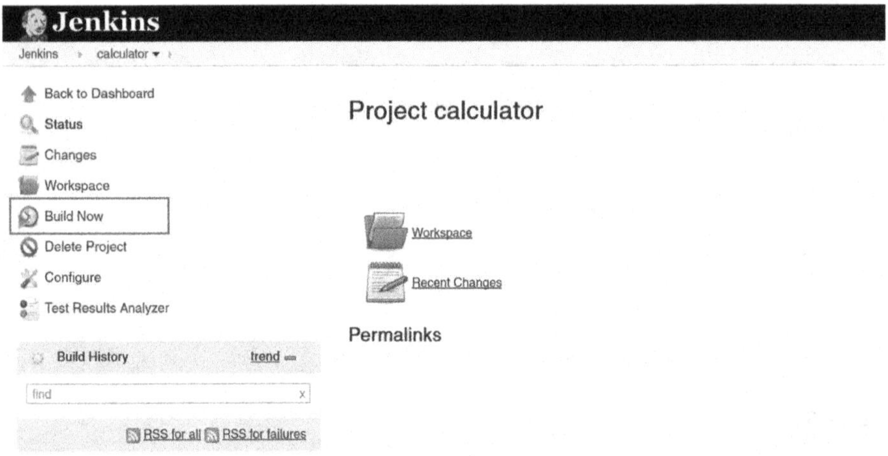
Jenkins
Jenkins
calculator
Back to Dashboard
Status
Changes
Workspace
Build Now
Delete Project
Configure
Test Results Analyzer
Build History
trend
find
RSS for all
RSS for failures
Project calculator
Workspace
Recent Changes
Permalinks

Figure 3-11. *Build now*

It helps, especially the first time, to see what's happening under the covers when Jenkins is building. Click on the build number so you can take look; see the number highlighted in Figure 3-12.

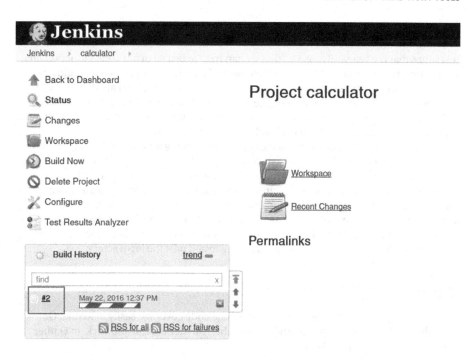

Figure 3-12. *Click on the Build number*

Click on Console Output to see if anything failed and where it broke in the build process, as shown in Figure 3-13. In this case, the build ran successfully.

Figure 3-13. *Jenkins console output*

Self-Verifying Unit Tests

Test suites that are self-verifying, i.e., that we can trust to test all of our code's functionality, are a critical piece of our test strategy. When we make a small change—such as add a new button—or change something more dramatic—such as changing from an MVC to a Clean Architecture—we want to have confidence in our tests that no functionality has changed and we haven't broken anything. After small or large changes, if all unit tests pass then we need to be confident that the end user will still have the same user experience.

Code coverage tells you how much of your code is being unit tested. It is a great way to visually see what code isn't being tested so you can rapidly fill in the gaps in your test suite.

Code coverage can also be a metric to tell you what percentage of the code has been covered with tests. If you're not calculating code coverage as a metric, you are flying blind. In the past I've seen people write unit tests on the login pages but then neglect to write unit tests for the app after the user is logged in. In that scenario, we cannot be sure that any new feature changes have not created any defects due to some unintended side effects in the existing code, as nothing was being tested past the login screen.

Slather

We saw in the previous chapter that we can enable code coverage easily in Xcode. Go to Product ➤ Scheme ➤ Edit Scheme, choose the Test Menu item, and click on Gather Code Coverage. See Figure 3-14.

Figure 3-14. *Adding code coverage in Xcode*

However, we want to be able to see the code coverage outside of the Xcode IDE so other people can view the metrics. We also want to be able to run it from the command line so we can add it as a step in our Jenkins build.

Slather is a third-party tool that allows us to take the Xcode metrics and display the coverage in a variety of options. It also works from the command line so we automate it using our continuous integration server.

Install Slather using the following command:

```
gem install slather
```

To output the code coverage in HTML, run the following command:

```
slather coverage --html --scheme XcodeSchemeName path/to/project.xcodeproj
```

For the Calculator code, this becomes:

```
slather coverage --html --scheme Calculator Calculator/Calculator.xcodeproj
```

The output is shown in Figure 3-15, which shows that there are no tests on the sub or mul methods.

Coverage for "CalculatorModel.swift" : 65.00%
(13 of 20 relevant lines covered)

Calculator/Calculator/CalculatorModel.swift

```
1   //
2   // CalculatorModel.swift
3   // Calculator
4   //
5   // Created by Admin on 4/16/16.
6   // Copyright © 2016 rils. All rights reserved.
7   //
8
9   import Foundation
10
11  class CalculatorModel {
12
13      var operandOne: Int
14      var operandTwo: Int
15
16      init(operandOne: Int, operandTwo: Int) {          5x
17          self.operandOne = operandOne                  5x
18          self.operandTwo = operandTwo                  5x
19      }                                                 6x
20
21      func add(operandOne: Int, operandTwo: Int) -> Int {   3x
22          return operandOne + operandTwo                    3x
23      }                                                     3x
24
25      func sub(operandOne: Int, operandTwo: Int) -> Int {   1
26          return operandOne - operandTwo                    1
27      }                                                     1
28
29      func mul(operandOne: Int, operandTwo: Int) -> Int {   1
30          return operandOne * operandTwo                    1
31      }                                                     1
32
33      func div(operandOne: Int, operandTwo: Int) -> Int {   1x
34                                                            1x
35          guard operandTwo != 0 else {                      1x
36              return 0                                      1x
37          }                                                 1x
38          return operandOne / operandTwo                    1
39      }                                                     1x
40
41  }
```

Figure 3-15. *Slather code coverage*

Technical Debt

Continuous integration (CI) servers such as Jenkins really come into their own when working on larger projects with a team of developers. As each developer checks in their code, the app is built and unit tested. You even have the option of letting the business stakeholder get a copy of the app using Testflight.

Experience will tell you that someone needs to be looking at the quality of the code to make sure your technical debt isn't getting out of control. Software projects all suffer from the Second Law of Thermodynamics, which states "that in every real process the sum of the entropies of all participating bodies is increased". Entropy is the chaos or disorder of a system, which as the law states, is always increasing. We can restate it for software engineering projects as follows: "in every software project the technical debt is always increasing".

There are ways to pay back the technical debt and decrease the entropy of your codebase, or in other words, increase its quality. Unfortunately, quality is too often a subjective measure in development teams. Code reviews can by their very nature be confrontational as people quite rightly are emotionally attached to their work. But there are other ways. There are tools that can make the code review process more objective and reduce the emotions on a team and get the team to focus on doing their job and delivering code. And thankfully we can automate these tools using our CI server.

We're going to look at three tools in this section. First there is Swift Lint, which is a third-party lint tool from Realm, second there is Swift Format, which removes any style questions from your code, and finally, there is SonarQube Swift Analyzer, which statically analyzes your code and performs and automated code reviews. All of these can be used within Jenkins.

Swift Lint

Make sure you install Homebrew. Go to `brew.sh` and run the ruby command to install. Once Homebrew is installed, you can go fetch and run `swiftlint` as follows:

```
$ brew install swiftlint
$ cd /path/to/XCode directory
$ swiftlint
```

Listing 3-5 shows the output of Swift Lint when we run it on the Calculator project.

Listing 3-5. Swift Lint First Run

```
$ swiftlint
Linting Swift files in current working directory
Linting 'AppDelegate.swift' (1/4)
/Users/Shared/Jenkins/Documents/Calculator/Calculator/AppDelegate.swift:46:
warning: Trailing Newline Violation: Files should have a single trailing
newline. (trailing_newline)
/Users/Shared/Jenkins/Documents/Calculator/Calculator/AppDelegate.swift:17:
warning: Line Length Violation: Line should be 100 characters or less:
currently 127 characters (line_length)
```

/Users/Shared/Jenkins/Documents/Calculator/Calculator/AppDelegate.swift:23:
error: Line Length Violation: Line should be 100 characters or less:
currently 285 characters (line_length)

.

.

.

Violation: Line should be 100 characters or less: currently 194 characters
(line_length)
/Users/Shared/Jenkins/Documents/Calculator/Calculator/AppDelegate.swift:41:
warning: Line Length Violation: Line should be 100 characters or less:
currently 128 characters (line_length)
Linting 'CalculatorModel.swift' (2/4)
/Users/Shared/Jenkins/Documents/Calculator/Calculator/CalculatorModel.
swift:41: warning: Trailing Newline Violation: Files should have a single
trailing newline. (trailing_newline)
/Users/Shared/Jenkins/Documents/Calculator/Calculator/CalculatorModel.
swift:16:22: warning: Opening Brace Spacing Violation: Opening braces should
be preceded by a single space and on the same line as the declaration.
(opening_brace)
/Users/Shared/Jenkins/Documents/Calculator/Calculator/CalculatorModel.
swift:16:10: warning: Colon Violation: Colons should be next to the
identifier when specifying a type. (colon)
/Users/Shared/Jenkins/Documents/Calculator/Calculator/CalculatorModel.
swift:16:17: warning: Colon Violation: Colons should be next to the
identifier when specifying a type. (colon)

.

.

.

Violation: Variable name should be between 3 and 40 characters long: 'b'
(variable_name)
/Users/Shared/Jenkins/Documents/Calculator/Calculator/CalculatorModel.
swift:33:14: error: Variable Name Violation: Variable name should be between
3 and 40 characters long: 'a' (variable_name)
/Users/Shared/Jenkins/Documents/Calculator/Calculator/CalculatorModel.
swift:33:21: error: Variable Name Violation: Variable name should be between
3 and 40 characters long: 'b' (variable_name)
/Users/Shared/Jenkins/Documents/Calculator/Calculator/CalculatorModel.
swift:12: warning: Trailing Whitespace Violation: Lines should not have
trailing whitespace. (trailing_whitespace)
/Users/Shared/Jenkins/Documents/Calculator/Calculator/CalculatorModel.
swift:15: warning: Trailing Whitespace Violation: Lines should not have
trailing whitespace. (trailing_whitespace)
/Users/Shared/Jenkins/Documents/Calculator/Calculator/CalculatorModel.
swift:20: warning: Trailing
Linting 'ViewController.swift' (3/4)
/Users/Shared/Jenkins/Documents/Calculator/Calculator/ViewController.
swift:75: warning: Trailing Newline Violation: Files should have a single
trailing newline. (trailing_newline)

/Users/Shared/Jenkins/Documents/Calculator/Calculator/ViewController.
swift:17:5: warning: Variable Name Violation: Variable name should be
between 3 and 40 characters long: 'op' (variable_name)
/Users/Shared/Jenkins/Documents/Calculator/Calculator/ViewController.
swift:60:9: warning: Control Statement Violation: if,for,while,do statements
shouldn't wrap their conditionals in parentheses. (control_statement)
/Users/Shared/Jenkins/Documents/Calculator/Calculator/ViewController.
swift:14: warning: Trailing Whitespace Violation: Lines should not have
trailing whitespace. (trailing_whitespace)
.

.

.

/Users/Shared/Jenkins/Documents/Calculator/Calculator/ViewController.
swift:67: warning: Trailing Whitespace Violation: Lines should not have
trailing whitespace. (trailing_whitespace)
Linting 'CalculatorTests.swift' (4/4)
/Users/Shared/Jenkins/Documents/Calculator/CalculatorTests/CalculatorTests.
swift:14:38: warning: Comma Spacing Violation: There should be no space
before and one after any comma. (comma)
/Users/Shared/Jenkins/Documents/Calculator/CalculatorTests/CalculatorTests.
swift:18:44: warning: Comma Spacing Violation: There should be no space
before and one after any comma. (comma)
/Users/Shared/Jenkins/Documents/Calculator/CalculatorTests/CalculatorTests.
swift:19:44: warning: Comma Spacing Violation: There should be no space
before and one after any comma. (comma)
/Users/Shared/Jenkins/Documents/Calculator/CalculatorTests/CalculatorTests.
swift:20:44: warning: Comma.
.

.

.

/Users/Shared/Jenkins/Documents/Calculator/CalculatorTests/CalculatorTests.
swift:25: warning: Trailing Whitespace Violation: Lines should not have
trailing whitespace. (trailing_whitespace)
/Users/Shared/Jenkins/Documents/Calculator/CalculatorTests/CalculatorTests.
swift:26: warning: Trailing Whitespace Violation: Lines should not have
trailing whitespace. (trailing_whitespace)
/Users/Shared/Jenkins/Documents/Calculator/CalculatorTests/CalculatorTests.
swift:27: warning: Trailing Whitespace Violation: Lines should not have
trailing whitespace. (trailing_whitespace)
Done linting! Found 66 violations, 14 serious in 4 files.

As you can see, there is lots of whitespace and many formatting errors. We can
manually fix them or we can get Swift Lint to correct the files if we run `swiftlint
autocorrect`. See Listing 3-6. Make sure to Git commit before taking this step in case you
need to reverse the changes.

Listing 3-6. Auto-Corrections

```
$ swiftlint autocorrect
Correcting Swift files in current working directory
Correcting 'AppDelegate.swift' (1/4)
/Users/Shared/Jenkins/Documents/Calculator/Calculator/AppDelegate.swift:45
Corrected Trailing Newline
Correcting 'CalculatorModel.swift' (2/4)
/Users/Shared/Jenkins/Documents/Calculator/Calculator/CalculatorModel.
swift:41 Corrected Trailing Newline
/Users/Shared/Jenkins/Documents/Calculator/Calculator/CalculatorModel.
swift:16:23 Corrected Opening Brace Spacing
/Users/Shared/Jenkins/Documents/Calculator/Calculator/CalculatorModel.
swift:33:21 Corrected Colon
/Users/Shared/Jenkins/Documents/Calculator/Calculator/CalculatorModel.
swift:33:14 Corrected Colon

.

.

.

Whitespace
/Users/Shared/Jenkins/Documents/Calculator/Calculator/CalculatorModel.
swift:40 Corrected Trailing Whitespace
Correcting 'ViewController.swift' (3/4)
/Users/Shared/Jenkins/Documents/Calculator/Calculator/ViewController.
swift:74 Corrected Trailing Newline
/Users/Shared/Jenkins/Documents/Calculator/Calculator/ViewController.
swift:14 Corrected Trailing.

.

.

.

/Users/Shared/Jenkins/Documents/Calculator/Calculator/ViewController.
swift:67 Corrected Trailing Whitespace
Correcting 'CalculatorTests.swift' (4/4)
/Users/Shared/Jenkins/Documents/Calculator/CalculatorTests/CalculatorTests.
swift:24:44 Corrected Comma Spacing
/Users/Shared/Jenkins/Documents/Calculator/CalculatorTests/CalculatorTests.
swift:20:44 Corrected Comma Spacing
/Users/Shared/Jenkins/Documents/Calculator/CalculatorTests/CalculatorTests.
swift:19:44 Corrected.

.

.

.

Done correcting 4 files!
```

If we run `swiftlint` again, we're down to 22 violations; see Listing 3-7.

Listing 3-7. Swiftlint Second Run

```
$ swiftlint
Linting Swift files in current working directory
Linting 'AppDelegate.swift' (1/4)
/Users/Shared/Jenkins/Documents/Calculator/Calculator/AppDelegate.swift:17:
warning: Line Length Violation: Line should be 100 characters or less:
currently 127 characters (line_length)
/Users/Shared/Jenkins/Documents/Calculator/Calculator/AppDelegate.swift:23:
error: Line Length Violation: Line should be 100 characters or less:
currently 285 characters (line_length)
/Users/Shared/Jenkins/Documents/Calculator/Calculator/AppDelegate.swift:24:
warning: Line Length Violation: Line should be 100 characters or less:
currently 155 characters (line_length)
/Users/Shared/Jenkins/Documents/Calculator/Calculator/AppDelegate.swift:28:
error: Line Length Violation: Line should be 100 characters or less:
currently 218 characters (line_length)
/Users/Shared/Jenkins/Documents/Calculator/Calculator/AppDelegate.swift:29:
warning: Line Length Violation: Line should be 100 characters or less:
currently 141 characters (line_length)
/Users/Shared/Jenkins/Documents/Calculator/Calculator/AppDelegate.swift:33:
warning: Line Length Violation: Line should be 100 characters or less:
currently 157 characters (line_length)
/Users/Shared/Jenkins/Documents/Calculator/Calculator/AppDelegate.swift:37:
warning: Line Length.
  .

  .

  .

/Users/Shared/Jenkins/Documents/Calculator/Calculator/CalculatorModel.
swift:33:14: error: Variable Name Violation: Variable name should be between
3 and 40 characters long: 'a' (variable_name)
/Users/Shared/Jenkins/Documents/Calculator/Calculator/CalculatorModel.
swift:33:22: error: Variable Name Violation: Variable name should be between
3 and 40 characters long: 'b' (variable_name)
Linting 'ViewController.swift' (3/4)
/Users/Shared/Jenkins/Documents/Calculator/Calculator/ViewController.
swift:17:5: warning: Variable Name Violation: Variable name should be
between 3 and 40 characters long: 'op' (variable_name)
/Users/Shared/Jenkins/Documents/Calculator/Calculator/ViewController.
swift:60:9: warning: Control Statement Violation: if,for,while,do statements
shouldn't wrap their conditionals in parentheses. (control_statement)
Linting 'CalculatorTests.swift' (4/4)
Done linting! Found 22 violations, 14 serious in 4 files.
```

Run your unit tests to make sure nothing has broken and check in the code. We can fix a lot of the lint errors by creating better variable names in our CalculatorModel code. See Listing 3-8. Use your favorite editor to do a find and replace on the two variables. As yet Xcode doesn't have any refactoring for Swift so we're going to have to manually make the fixes.

Listing 3-8. Updated CalculatorModel Code to Fix Lint Issues

```swift
import Foundation

class CalculatorModel {

    var operandOne: Int
    var operandTwo: Int

    init() {
    }

    func add(operandOne: Int, operandTwo: Int) -> Int {
        return operandOne + operandTwo
    }

    func sub(operandOne: Int, operandTwo: Int) -> Int {
        return operandOne - operandTwo
    }

    func mul(operandOne: Int, operandTwo: Int) -> Int {
        return operandOne * operandTwo
    }

    func div(operandOne: Int, operandTwo: Int) -> Int {
        guard operandTwo != 0 else {
            return 0
        }
        return operandOne / operandTwo
    }

}
```

Get the code to compile again, run your unit tests and, if they all pass, then check the code in. The AppDelegate.swift code is autogenerated Xcode, so we can ignore it or (better still) clear it up by removing the comments. We should also look at the ViewController.swift warning.

```
Linting 'ViewController.swift' (3/4)
/Users/Shared/Jenkins/Documents/Calculator/Calculator/ViewController.
swift:60:9: warning: Control Statement Violation: if,for,while,do statements
shouldn't wrap their conditionals in parentheses. (control_statement)
```

If that's not something you view as important then you can disable the checking by adding the following to the .swiftlint.yml file. See Listing 3-9.

Listing 3-9. .swiftlint.yml File

```
disabled_rules:
 - control_statement
```

Run lint again. Now there are no errors in the files, as shown in Listing 3-10.

Listing 3-10. Swift Lint Third Run

```
$ swiftlint
Linting Swift files in current working directory
Linting 'AppDelegate.swift' (1/4)
Linting 'CalculatorModel.swift' (2/4)
Linting 'ViewController.swift' (3/4)
Linting 'CalculatorTests.swift' (4/4)
Done linting! Found 0 violations, 0 serious in 4 files.
```

We can add Swift Lint as a build step in Jenkins. Click on the Jenkins project and choose Configure. Scroll down to add Build Step ➤ Execute Shell and then add the full path to Swift Lint. See Figure 3-16.

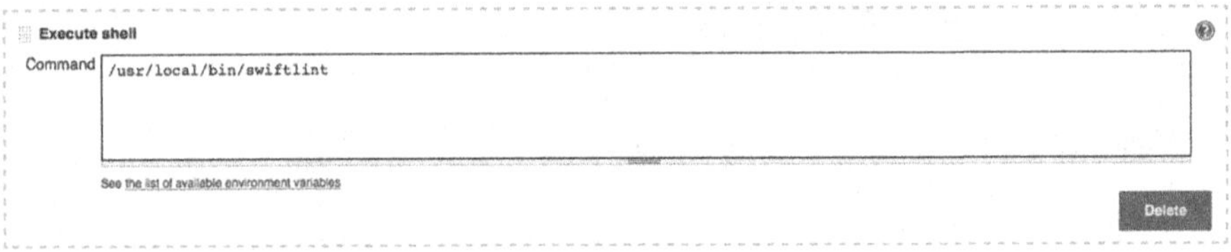

Figure 3-16. *Running Swift Lint within Jenkins*

Swift Format

One of the goals of this book and this chapter is to use tools that make the development process more objective and less subjective. Too much time has been lost discussing whether you should use indents or tabs in your code. Some people can get very worked up about indents versus tabs or where to put their curly braces or how many lines to leave between a method declaration and the variables. These sort of discussions can unnecessarily prolong code reviews. Time can be spent more productively writing code rather than arguing over its formatting. The requirement is surely to be consistent across the entire codebase.

SwiftFormat can provide this consistency across your codebase. Assuming that everyone can agree on the basic rules for how you want your code to look, SwiftFormat can apply those rules programmatically. At worst you're only going to have the indents versus tabs argument once now before you code the rules in SwiftFormat.

SwiftFormat provides rules for the following Swift coding styles. There is no reason why you can't add your own rules by extending the code.

- Line breaks

- Semicolons

- Specifiers

- Braces

- ElseOnSameLine

- Indent

- Space

- ConsecutiveSpaces

- BlankLinesAtEndOfScope

- BlankLinesBetweenScopes

- ConsecutiveBlankLines

- TrailingWhitespace

- LinebreakAtEndOfFile

- TrailingCommas

- Todos

- Ranges

Download SwiftFormat from `https://github.com/nicklockwood/SwiftFormat`. Run the command `swiftformat -i 4` against your Swift file or directory for code that you want indented with four spaces.

As an example, let's take a look at the before and after for some code that mocks out the iOS AudioPlayer. Listing 3-11 shows the before function.

Listing 3-11. testIncreaseAudioVolume before SwiftFormat

```
func testIncreaseAudioplayerVolume()
{
    let mock = MockAVAudioPlayerHelper()
    let mockPlayerProtocol = MockAVAudioPlayerProtocol()

    let url = NSURL.fileURL(withPath: Bundle.main.path(forResource:
    "Sample", of Type: "mp3")!) let _: NSError?
    var tempAudioPlayer: AVAudioPlayer?

    do
    {
        try
            tempAudioPlayer = AVAudioPlayer(contentsOf: url)
    } catch
```

```
    {
        print("audioPlayer error \(error.localizedDescription)")
    }
    tempAudioPlayer?.volume = 1.0

    XCTAssertEqual(mock.audioPlayer?.volume,1.0)
    XCTAssertEqual(mock.getVolume,1.0)
    XCTAssertEqual(mock.audioPlayer?.volume,tempAudioPlayer?.volume)
}
```

Run `swiftformat -i 4` on the code. You'll see that the formatting has fixed the do-try-catch to something that most developers would expect to see. Although the differences are subtle, it makes the code tidier and more professional looking; see Listing 3-12.

Listing 3-12. testIncreaseAudioVolume after SwiftFormat

```
func testIncreaseAudioplayerVolume() {
    let mock = MockAVAudioPlayerHelper()
    let mockPlayerProtocol = MockAVAudioPlayerProtocol()

    let url = NSURL.fileURL(withPath: Bundle.main.path(forResource:
    "Sample", of Type: "mp3")!) let _: NSError?
    var tempAudioPlayer: AVAudioPlayer?

    do {
        try
            tempAudioPlayer = AVAudioPlayer(contentsOf: url)
    } catch {
        print("audioPlayer error \(error.localizedDescription)")
    }
    tempAudioPlayer?.volume = 1.0

    XCTAssertEqual(mock.audioPlayer?.volume, 1.0)
    XCTAssertEqual(mock.getVolume, 1.0)
    XCTAssertEqual(mock.audioPlayer?.volume, tempAudioPlayer?.volume)
}
```

SonarQube

Lint is a great first step, but it's only a first step. We said earlier that we're trying to move from a subjective analysis or code review to an objective one and there are many tools other than Lint that can do a more detailed job of static code analysis. SonarQube is one such tool that can grade your code. It can calculate metrics for complexity, the security of the code, and the amount of time you're going to need to pay back the technical debt on your code. See Figure 3-17. Unfortunately, the Swift static code analyzer on SonarQube isn't free but it's still worth looking at.

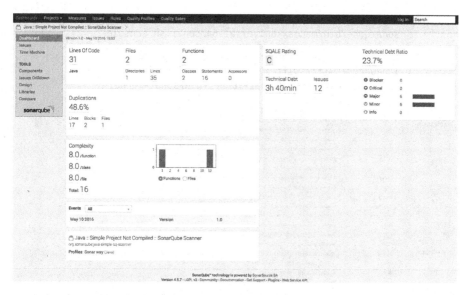

***Figure 3-17.** SonarQube dashboard*

Install SonarQube

To install SonarQube, take the following steps:

1. Download SonarQube from http://www.sonarqube.org/
   downloads and unzip the SonarQube distribution into /etc/
   sonarqube.

2. Download SonarQube scanner from https://sonarsource.
   bintray.com/Distribution/sonar-scanner-cli/sonar-
   scanner-2.6.1.zip and install it in /etc/sonar-runner.

3. Log in to SonarQube at http://localhost:9090 (assuming
   you're on the CI server) with the default system administrator
   credentials, which are admin/admin.

4. Go to Settings ➤ Update Center ➤ Available Plugins ➤
   Languages ➤ Swift and install the Swift plugin
   (see Figure 3-18).

5. Once the plugin is installed, click on Installed Plugins in the
   Update Center.

6. Go to Settings ➤ General Settings ➤ Licenses.

7. Enter the license key in the Swift field and click Save Licenses
   Settings.

8. Download the SonarQube examples from https://github.
   com/SonarSource/sonar-examples/archive/master.zip and
   unzip it in /etc/sonar-examples.

9. In one terminal on the CI server, start the console sudo /etc/sonarqube/bin/macosx-universal-64/sonar.sh console.

10. In another terminal cd to /etc/sonar-examples/project/languages/swift/swift-sonar-runner and run the sonar-runner as follows: /etc/sonar-runner/bin/sonar-runner.

Figure 3-18. *Install Swift plugin*

The sample Swift code is shown in Listing 3-13. It's very simple but at least it will tell us if the Swift plugin is working.

Listing 3-13. SonarQube example.swift Code

```
let names = ["Chris", "Alex", "Ewa", "Barry", "Daniella"]

func backwards(s1: String, s2: String) -> Bool {
    return s1 > s2
}

var reversed = sorted(names, backwards);

if (true) { print(reversed) }
```

Go back to the Dashboard, http://localhost:9090, and click on the Swift project. See Figure 3-19. You should see a new dashboard for your project. We're doing great—our project is getting an A in the Software Quality Assessment based on the Lifecycle Expectations metric or SQALE. We also only have a couple of issues. Click on the number under issues to see more.

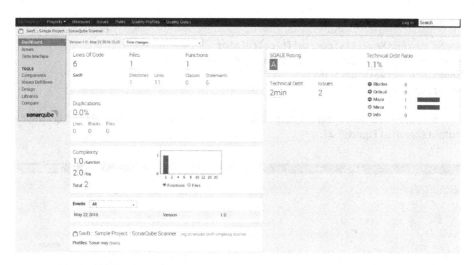

Figure 3-19. An example.swift dashboard

Click on the `example.swift` file to drill down into the issues at a code level. The SonarQube major issue is we should not put more than one statement on a line. See Figure 3-20.

Figure 3-20. SonarQube example.swift Code issues

Now we're ready to try it on our Calculator project.

Add the Calculator Project

Add `sonar.projectKey`, `projectName`, and `projectVersion` to the `sonar.properties` class and use the `sources` property to tell it where to find the code. See Listing 3-14.

Listing 3-14. The sonar.properties File

```
sonar.projectKey=riis.com:swift-calculator
sonar.projectName=Swift :: Calculator Project
sonar.projectVersion=1.0
sonar.sources=Calculator
```

Execute /etc/sonar-runner/bin/sonar-scanner in a terminal. You should get the output shown in Figure 3-21.

Figure 3-21. SonarQube dashboard for the Calculator app

If you click on the errors, you can see that they are minimal and easily fixed. See Figure 3-22.

Figure 3-22. SonarQube issues for the Calculator app

Fix the code using SonarQube and rerun the Calculator tests to make sure nothing is broken. Finally, rerun the scanner to show there are no more major issues.

Adding SonarQube to Jenkins

SonarQube can also run as part of your Jenkins build. From the Jenkins Dashboard, choose Manage Jenkins ➤ Manage Plugins ➤ Available. Search for and install the SonarQube plugin. Restart the server.

To configure your existing SonarQube server so Jenkins can see it, choose Manage Jenkins ➤ Configure System. Scroll down to SonarQube servers, choose a name for your SonarQube install, and enter a server URL—ideally a fully qualified domain name, as shown in Figure 3-23.

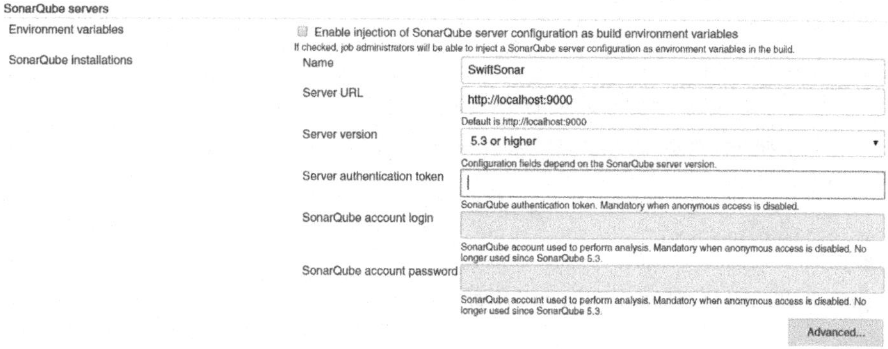

Figure 3-23. *SonarQube server configuration on Jenkins*

Scroll down to the SonarQube scanner and add a name for your SonarQube instance. Unclick the Install Automatically checkbox, add SONAR_RUNNER_HOME, and click Save. See Figure 3-24.

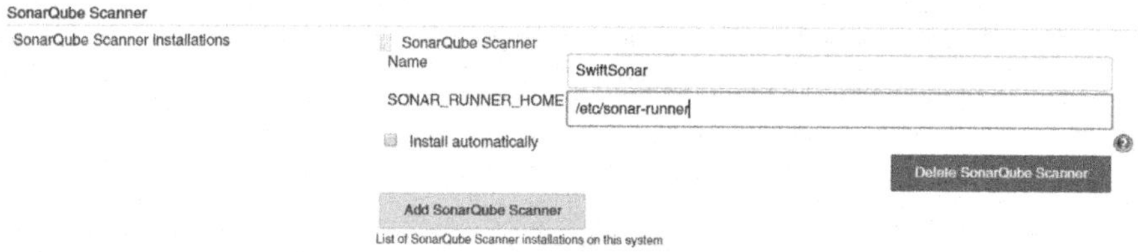

Figure 3-24. *SonarQube scanner configuration on Jenkins*

91

Adding SonarQube to Calculator Jenkins Project

Where SonarQube and Jenkins really shine is that they provide the ability for anyone with access to the Jenkins server to check in from time to time and see if the project quality is still on track. To set this up in Jenkins, click on the project name in the Dashboard, click on Configure, and scroll down to the Add Build step. Add Execute SonarQube Scanner, as shown in Figure 3-25.

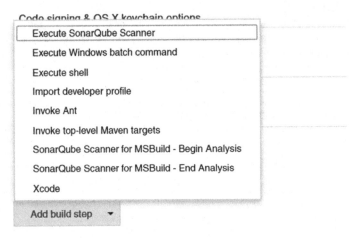

Figure 3-25. Add the SonarQube build step

Scroll down to Execute SonarQube Scanner and add the path to your SonarQube project properties file, as shown in Figure 3-26. This is the same properties file shown earlier in Listing 3-14.

Figure 3-26. Add the sonar-project.properties file

Click on Build Now to build the project. If everything works, you should be able to see your project's SonarQube dashboard by clicking on the SonarQube link, which now appears on your Project Dashboard. See Figure 3-27.

Project calculator

SonarQube

Workspace

Recent Changes

SonarQube Quality Gate

Figure 3-27. Link to the SonarQube Dashboard

The Dashboard for the Calculator project is the same one you saw earlier in Figure 3-21. Thankfully we're still getting an A and, while there are a number of major issues, they turn out to be more formatting issues similar to the sample project. There are no blocker or critical issues.

Stevia

We'll see in Chapter 6 when we talk about TDD that Swift programming on the iOS platform has to deal with too much user interface scaffolding for the developer to ever develop a good red/green/refactor cadence. The problem is that to create a mobile app, the developer has to keep switching between writing code and creating the interface in the Interface Builder and back again.

The Interface Builder generates code based on your interactions, so it should be possible to create the same code without ever having to touch the Interface Builder. Unfortunately, the overhead to write the Auto Layout code generated by the Interface Builder is almost as time consuming as using the Interface Builder to do it for you. Auto Layout has a relatively steep learning curve and increases your code complexity. However, there are third-party tools that dramatically simplify this process.

We're going to look at how Stevia can help you get the TDD cadence back. Stevia is one of several auto layout Domain Specific Languages or DSLs and aims to make the auto layout code readable.

Listing 3-15 shows an example of how to code the layout in Stevia.

Listing 3-15. Stevia Layout

```
layout(
    100,
```

```
  |-email-| ~ 80,
  8,
  |-password-| ~ 80,
  "",
  |login| ~ 80,
  0
)
```

Figure 3-28 shows the interface generated from this Layout.

Figure 3-28. *Stevia Login screen*

To install Stevia, take the following steps:

1. Run pod init on the project's top-level directory.

2. Add the following to the generated podfile:

    ```
    pod 'SteviaLayout'
    use_frameworks!
    ```

We'll look at Stevia again later in this book.

Summary

In this chapter, we looked at a number of third-party tools to complement the XCTest for improved unit testing. We looked at Nimble to help expand our assertions or create our own; we looked briefly at how to use Cuckoo for mocking to isolate our tests; we looked at Jenkins for our continuous integration needs; we looked at Slather to measure our code coverage; and finally we looked at Swift Lint and SonarQube to measure the code quality. Every tool either runs from the command line or is integrated within Jenkins. This means we have a much better chance of maintaining the quality and the life of each project long into the future.

CHAPTER 4

Mocking

One of the major goals, whether it's on the iOS platform or not, is to isolate the code that we're testing. When we write our tests, we want to test a specific class's method without any of the associated interactions with other classes in the app or any external elements, such as a web service. We should be testing a single method, not its dependencies. This method should also be the only code covered by the test, with everything else mocked.

Mocking out these third-party interactions is a great way to put a fence around a method so we're not reliant on such things as the network, a device's location, or local time when we're doing our testing. The only reason a test should fail is because there's something wrong with the code, never because external dependencies (such as the WiFi) are not working.

Mocking dependencies allows you to get your tests to run quicker than the alternative, which often means having to wait for the simulator to start or the network to respond. Sure, there are times when you need to use a simulator, such as when you're testing Views, but you'll see in the next chapter how this can be accomplished better using the XCUI framework rather than in XCTest.

In this chapter, we'll start with our simple Hello World example and then look at how we can mock out the following interactions to achieve test isolation and faster test execution.

- HTTP calls
- User defaults
- Dates
- Audio player

Same Rules Do Not Apply

Mocking in Swift isn't the same as in other languages. There aren't any predominant Mocking frameworks, such as OCMock in Objective-C or Mockito in Java. Other languages can use reflection to alter runtime code to mock out the classes. But you can't do that in Swift. It's been designed to be a much safer language and doesn't allow the code to be modified at runtime. So you're going to have think a little differently to achieve the same results as say OCMock. The language is also so new and is changing so rapidly that there isn't a stable, mature mocking framework that you can rely on to be updated for Swift 3, let alone future versions of Swift.

© Godfrey Nolan 2017
G. Nolan, *Agile Swift*, DOI 10.1007/978-1-4842-2102-0_4

Cuckoo

Currently there *is* a mocking framework called Cuckoo that will allow us to mock out our code similar to OCMock. Cuckoo is a two-stage mocking framework and is available from https://github.com/SwiftKit/Cuckoo. The first part, CuckooGenerator, scans your code and creates a GeneratedMocks.swift file, which you then write your test mocks against. When you run your tests, the GeneratedMocks.swift code, together with the Cuckoo library, enable your mocks to function as you would expect.

Let's start with a simple Hello, World! example to see how it works. Because it's a two-stage process, it isn't seamless, but we have enough examples in the chapter that it should become second nature.

Listing 4-1 shows the sayIt() function, which returns the Hello, World! string.

Listing 4-1. Hello World!

```
class Hello
{
    func sayIt() -> String
    {
        return "Hello, World!"
    }
}
```

For our purposes, we want the mock to return a different string when the sayIt() function is called. We saw in the last chapter that we can summarize how we use mocks as follows:

```
when(methodIsCalled).thenReturn(aValue);
```

When our method or function is called, it should return our canned value. So we want our mocked code to be as follows:

```
mock.sayIt().thenReturn("Hello,How are you")
```

To install Cuckoo, follow these steps:

1. Create your project with the Hello.swift model class and test class.

2. Install the Cuckoo pod by first running pod init from the command line.

3. Edit the generated podfile and add Cuckoo as a test target, as shown in Listing 4-2.

Listing 4-2. Podfile

```
target 'HelloWorldCuckooTests' do
    pod 'Cuckoo',
    :git => 'https://github.com/SwiftKit/Cuckoo.git',
    :branch => 'master'
end
```

4. Run the pod install command.

5. Close the project and reopen the workspace.

6. Click on the Project folder and choose Test Target->Build Phases.

7. Click + and choose New Run Script Phase.

8. Add Listing 4-3 to the Run Script section.

9. Build the project.

Listing 4-3. Cuckoo Run Script

```
# Define output file; change "${PROJECT_NAME}Tests" to your test's root
source folder, if it's not the default name
OUTPUT_FILE="./${PROJECT_NAME}Tests/GeneratedMocks.swift"
echo "Generated Mocks File = ${OUTPUT_FILE}"

# Define input directory; change "${PROJECT_NAME}" to your project's root
source folder, if it's not the default name
INPUT_DIR="./${PROJECT_NAME}"
echo "Mocks Input Directory = ${INPUT_DIR}"

# Generate mock files; include as many input files as you'd like to create
mocks for
${PODS_ROOT}/Cuckoo/run generate --testable "${PROJECT_NAME}" \
--output "${OUTPUT_FILE}" \
"${INPUT_DIR}/Hello.swift"
```

10. Right-click on HelloWorldCuckooTests and add GeneratorModel.swift to the test folder, as shown in Figure 4-1.

Figure 4-1. *Add GeneratorMock.swift to your test folder*

11. Create the mock in HelloWorldCuckooTests, as shown in Listing 4-4.

12. Run the mocked tests.

Listing 4-4. Mocked HelloWorld

```
func testSayItIsntSo() {

    let mock = MockHello()

    stub(mock, block: { (mock) in
        mock.sayIt().thenReturn("Hello,How are you")
    })

    XCTAssertEqual(mock.sayIt(), "Hello,How are you")
}
```

Figure 4-2 shows the test results.

Tests	Coverage	Logs

All	Passed	Failed	All	Performance		⊙ Filter
Tests						Status
▼ HelloWorldCuckooTests › HelloWorldCuckooTests						
🔲 testSayItIsntSo()						◈

Figure 4-2. *testSayItIsntSo results*

Mocking HTTP

Unit tests should be isolated from any network calls. We want whatever our code is doing with the URL or REST API to be hidden from any network issues when we are unit testing our code. We would test that when we're doing integration testing. Listing 4-5 shows the UrlSession class code, which does a simple GET for a given URL.

Listing 4-5. UrlSession.swift Code

```
class UrlSession
{
    var url:URL?
    var session:URLSession?
    var apiUrl:String?

    func getSourceUrl(apiUrl:String) -> URL
    {
        url = URL(string:apiUrl)
        return url!
    }

    func callApi(url:URL) -> String
    {
        session = URLSession()
        var outputdata:String = ""
        let task = session?.dataTask(with: url as URL) { (data, _, _) ->
        Void in
            if let data = data
            {
                outputdata = String(data: data, encoding: String.Encoding.
                utf8)!
                print(outputdata)

            }
        }

        task?.resume()

        return outputdata

    }
}
```

Ideally we would want to mock this out so we get a specific string of canned HTML or JSON text that we can then manipulate, parse, or deconstruct in our application and test how these functions work.

To install Cuckoo, follow these steps:

1. Create your UrlWithCuckoo project with the UrlSession. swift model class and test class.

2. Install the Cuckoo pod by first running pod init from the command line.

3. Edit the generated podfile and then add Cuckoo as a test target, as shown in Listing 4-2.

4. Run the pod install command.

5. Close the project and reopen the workspace.

6. Click on the Project folder and choose Test Target ➤ Build Phases.

7. Click + and choose New Run Script Phase.

8. Add Listing 4-6 to the Run Script section.

9. Build the project.

Listing 4-6. Cuckoo Run Script

```
# Define output file; change "${PROJECT_NAME}Tests" to your test's root
source folder, if it's not the default name
OUTPUT_FILE="./${PROJECT_NAME}Tests/GeneratedMocks.swift"
echo "Generated Mocks File = ${OUTPUT_FILE}"

# Define input directory; change "${PROJECT_NAME}" to your project's root
source folder, if it's not the default name
INPUT_DIR="./${PROJECT_NAME}"
echo "Mocks Input Directory = ${INPUT_DIR}"

# Generate mock files; include as many input files as you'd like to create
mocks for
${PODS_ROOT}/Cuckoo/run generate --testable "${PROJECT_NAME}" \
--output "${OUTPUT_FILE}" \
"${INPUT_DIR}/UrlSession.swift"
```

10. Right-click on UrlWithCuckooTests and add GeneratorModel.swift to the test folder, as shown in Figure 4-1.

11. Using the newly available functions from GeneratorModel. swift, mock out the getSourceURL and callAPI function calls.

Listing 4-7 shows the mocked code that returns a simple but valid string of an HTML web page. We mock out the two function calls—the first determines whether getSourceURL returns a mock URL and the second determines whether callAPI returns a simple JSON string.

Listing 4-7. testURL() Session Code

```swift
func testUrl()
    {
        let mock = MockUrlSession()
        let urlStr  = "http://riis.com"
        let url  = URL(string:urlStr)!

        stub(mock)
        { (mock) in

            when(mock.apiUrl).get.thenReturn(urlStr)
        }

        stub(mock)
        { (mock) in

            when(mock.url).get.thenReturn(url)
        }

        stub(mock)
        { (mock) in

            when(mock.session).get.thenReturn(URLSession())
        }
        stub(mock) { (stub) in
            stub.getSourceUrl(apiUrl: urlStr).thenReturn(url)
        }

        stub(mock) { mock in
            mock.callApi(url: equal(to:url, equalWhen: { $0 == $1 })).
            thenReturn("{'firstName': 'John','lastName': 'Smith'}")

        }

        XCTAssertNotNil(verify(mock).session)
        XCTAssertNotNil(verify(mock).apiUrl)
        XCTAssertNotNil(verify(mock).url)

        XCTAssertEqual(mock.apiUrl, urlStr)
        XCTAssertEqual(mock.url?.absoluteString, urlStr)
        XCTAssertNotNil(mock.session)
        XCTAssertEqual(mock.callApi(url: url),"{'firstName':
        'John','lastName': 'Smith'}")

    }
```

We run the test code and the results can be seen in Figure 4-3.

Figure 4-3. *testURL results*

Mocking User Defaults

Our sample app for this use case is shown in Figure 4-4. It takes a user's username, password, and date of birth.

Figure 4-4. *Username, password, and date of birth*

Name:	godfreynolan
DOB:	Mar 1, 1966
Age:	You are 50 years old now

Figure 4-5. *Detail view of the saved data*

User defaults or NSUserDefaults are built-in iOS functionalities, meaning that we don't need to test them. When testing our app we will want to test our code using a fake username so we don't have to get someone to log in to the app to test other methods.

Listing 4-8. User Model Code

```
import Foundation

class UserDefaultsMock
{
    var standardUserDefaults :UserDefaults?

    init(suiteName:String)
    {
        standardUserDefaults = UserDefaults.standard
        standardUserDefaults?.addSuite(named: suiteName)
        standardUserDefaults?.synchronize()
    }
}
```

It would be useful if we could set the name and user ID of the user so that we don't have to log in each time we're testing the app if we want to test any subsequent logic.

To install Cuckoo, follow these steps:

1. Create your Date project with the UserDefaultsMock.swift model class and test classes.

2. Install the Cuckoo pod by first running pod init from the command line.

3. Edit the generated podfile and then add Cuckoo as a test target, as shown in Listing 4-2.

4. Run the pod install command.

5. Close the project and reopen the workspace.

6. Click on the Project folder and choose Test Target ➤ Build Phases.

7. Click + and choose New Run Script Phase.

8. Add Listing 4-6 to the Run Script section and change UrlSession.swift to UserDefaultsWithCuckoo.swift.

9. Build the project.

10. Right-click on UserDefaultsWithCuckoo and add GeneratorModel.swift to the test folder, similar to Figure 4-1.

11. Using the newly available functions from GeneratorModel.swift, we create mock classes for testUserDefaults, testGetFirstnameFromDefaults, testGetAmountValueFromDefaults, and testGetUserIdValueFromDefaults.

Listing 4-9 shows the mock code. In the code, we create the user-default objects and set up the mocks in setUp().

Listing 4-9. User Mock Code

```
import XCTest
import Cuckoo

@testable import UserDefaultsWithCuckoo

class UserDefaultsWithCuckooTests: XCTestCase
{
    let suiteName = "UnitTestingUserDefaults"
    var mock:MockUserDefaultsMock!

    override func setUp()
    {
        super.setUp()
```

```
    // Put setup code here. This method is called before the invocation
    of each test method in the class.

    mock = MockUserDefaultsMock(suiteName: suiteName)
    stub(mock) {
        (mock) in
        when(mock.standardUserDefaults.get).thenReturn(UserDefaults.
        standard)
    }

}

override func tearDown()
{
    // Put teardown code here. This method is called after the
    invocation of each test method in the class.
    super.tearDown()

    mock.standardUserDefaults?.removeSuite(named: suiteName)
    reset(mock)
}

func testUserDefaults()
{
    XCTAssertNotNil(mock.standardUserDefaults)
    XCTAssertNotNil(verify(mock).standardUserDefaults)

}

func testGetFirstnameFromDefaults()
{
    mock.standardUserDefaults?.set("SwiftUser", forKey: "Firstname")
    XCTAssertEqual(mock.standardUserDefaults?.value(forKey: "Firstname")
    as! String,"SwiftUser")
}

func testGetAmountValueFromDefaults()
{
    mock.standardUserDefaults?.set(100.0, forKey: "amount")
    XCTAssertEqual(mock.standardUserDefaults?.float(forKey: "amount"),100.0)
}

func testGetUserIdValueFromDefaults()
{
    mock.standardUserDefaults?.set(8, forKey: "UserId")
    XCTAssertEqual(mock.standardUserDefaults?.integer(forKey: "UserId"),8)
}

}
```

Run the tests on these simple mocks; the results are shown in Figure 4-6.

	Tests	Coverage	Logs	
All Passed Failed All Performance				⊕ Filter
Tests				Status
▼ UserDefaultsWuthCuckooTests › UserDefaultsWuthCuckooTests				
testGetUserIdValueFromDefaults()				✓
testGetAmountValueFromDefaults()				✓
testUserDefaults()				✓
testGetFirstnameFromDefaults()				✓

Figure 4-6. *Test results*

Mocking Date and Time

If we add a birth date to our User class, we can show how to create our own iOS date/time environment. This abstraction allows us to hide the implementation so that we can control time zones and day of the year and create a lot more edge case tests to give our code a workout. When we test our code, we can use a mock date/time implementation to make our job easier.

The data is saved and displayed on the next view, shown in Figure 4-5. If it happens to be your birthday, you will get a pop-up message wishing you a happy birthday.

Listing 4-10 shows the DateImplementation code with functions for checking the previous and current month, calculating the person's age, and determining whether it's the user's birthday. If it is her birthday, it creates a pop-up message wishing the user a happy birthday.

Listing 4-10. DateImplementation.swift

```swift
class DateImplementation
{
    var chosenDate : Date?

    func getPreviousMonth() -> Int
    {
        let cal = Calendar.autoupdatingCurrent

        return cal.component(.month, from: cal.date(byAdding: .month, value:
        -1, to: self.chosenDate!)!)
    }

    func getCurrentMonth() -> Int
    {
        let cal = Calendar.autoupdatingCurrent

        return cal.component(.month, from: cal.date(byAdding: .month,
        value:0, to: self.chosenDate!)!)
    }
```

```swift
func calculateAge() -> Int
{
    let calendar = NSCalendar.current
    let ageComponents = calendar.dateComponents([.year,.month,.day],
    from:self.chosenDate!, to:NSDate() as Date)
    let personAge = ageComponents.year

    return personAge!

}

func checkForBirthday() -> Bool
{
    let dateFormatter = DateFormatter()
    dateFormatter.dateStyle = DateFormatter.Style.medium

    let currentDate = Date()

    dateFormatter.dateFormat = "MMM"
    let month = dateFormatter.string(from: chosenDate!)
    let currentMonth = dateFormatter.string(from: currentDate)

    dateFormatter.dateFormat = "dd"
    let day = dateFormatter.string(from: chosenDate!)
    let currentDay = dateFormatter.string(from: currentDate)

    if currentDay == day && currentMonth == month
    {
        return true
    }
    else
    {
        return false
    }
}
}
```

It would be useful if we could set the date to match a user's birthday by mocking the date and calling checkForBirthday(). We have no control over the date, so it's an obvious place to mock.

To install Cuckoo, follow these steps:

1. Create your Date project with the DateImplementation.swift model class and test classes.

2. Install the Cuckoo pod by first running pod init from the command line.

3. Edit the generated podfile and then add Cuckoo as a test target, as shown in Listing 4-2.

4. Run the pod install command.

5. Close the project and reopen the workspace.

6. Click on the Project folder and then choose Test Target ➤ Build Phases.

7. Click + and choose New Run Script Phase.

8. Add Listing 4-6 to the Run Script section and change UrlSession.swift to DateImplementation.swift.

9. Build the project.

10. Right-click on DateWithCuckooTests and add GeneratorModel.swift to the test folder, similar to Figure 4-1.

11. Using the newly available functions from GeneratorModel. swift, we mock calculateAge, getCurrentMonth, getPreviousMonth, and checkForBirthday.

Listing 4-11 shows the mock code. In the code, we create the Date objects and set up the mocks in setUp().

Listing 4-11. DateImplementationTests.swift

```swift
import XCTest
import Cuckoo

@testable import DateWithCuckoo

class DateImplementationTests: XCTestCase
{
    var previousYearDate: Date?
    var mock:MockDateImplementation!
    var mockedDate :Date!

    override func setUp()
    {
        super.setUp()

        let calendar = Calendar.autoupdatingCurrent

        let previousYear = calendar.component(.year, from: calendar.
        date(byAdding: .year, value: -3, to: Date())!)
        let currentMonth = calendar.component(.month, from: calendar.
        date(byAdding: .month, value: 0, to: Date())!)
        let currentDay = calendar.component(.day, from: calendar.
        date(byAdding: .day, value: 0, to: Date())!)

        let mockDateAndTime = MockDateAndTime()
```

```
    previousYearDate = mockDateAndTime.from(previousYear, month:
    currentMonth, day: currentDay) as Date
    mockedDate = mockDateAndTime.from(2014, month: 05, day: 20) as Date

    mock = MockDateImplementation().spy(on: DateImplementation())

    stub(mock) {
        (mock) in
        when(mock.chosenDate.get).thenReturn(mockedDate!)
    }

    stub(mock) { mock in

        when(mock.calculateAge()).thenReturn(3)
    }

stub(mock) { mock in

        mock.checkForBirthday().thenReturn(true)

    }

    stub(mock) { mock in
      when(mock.getCurrentMonth()).thenReturn(05)
    }

    stub(mock) { mock in
            when(mock.getPreviousMonth()).thenReturn(04)
    }
}

class MockDateAndTime
{
    func from(_ year:Int, month:Int, day:Int) -> Date
    {
        var c = DateComponents()
        c.year = year
        c.month = month
        c.day = day

        let gregorian = Calendar(identifier:Calendar.Identifier.
        gregorian)
        let date = gregorian.date(from: c as DateComponents)

        return (date! as NSDate) as Date
    }
}
```

```swift
    override func tearDown()
    {
        // Put teardown code here. This method is called after the
        invocation of each test method in the class.
        super.tearDown()
        self.previousYearDate = nil
        self.mockedDate = nil
        reset(mock!)
    }

    func testDateVerify()
    {
        XCTAssertNotNil(mock.chosenDate)
        XCTAssertEqual(mock.chosenDate, mockedDate)
        XCTAssertNotNil(verify(mock).chosenDate)
    }

    func testGetMonths()
    {
        let currentMonth = mock.getCurrentMonth()
        let previousMonth = mock.getPreviousMonth()

        XCTAssertEqual(currentMonth,05)
        XCTAssertEqual(previousMonth,04)
    }

    func testAge()
    {
        let age = mock.calculateAge()

        XCTAssertNotNil(age)
        XCTAssertNotEqual(age, 2)
        XCTAssertEqual(age, 3)
    }

    func testForBirthDay()
    {
        let birthday = mock.checkForBirthDay()

        XCTAssertEqual(birthday, true)
    }

}
```

Now that we've mocked the date, we verify that it's set correctly in testDateVerify() and also test the user's age in testAge(). Finally, we assert that the user's birthday is today using testForBirthDay().

The test results are shown in Figure 4-7.

			Tests	Coverage	Logs		

All	Passed	Failed	All	Performance		⊙ Filter
Tests						**Status**
▼ DateImplementationTests › DateWithCuckooTests						
🔳 testDateVerify()						✓
🔳 testGetMonths()						✓
🔳 testAge()						✓
🔳 testForBirthDay()						✓

Figure 4-7. *DateImplementationTests.swift test results*

Mocking System Settings

We can take the same approach with system settings. In this final example, we show how to set the media player volume by mocking out the system settings. Listing 4-12 shows the code for the AVAudioPlayerHelper class. The model code has the getVolume() and increaseVolumeofAudioPlayer() functions.

Listing 4-12. AVAudioPlayerHelper.swift

```swift
import Foundation
import AVFoundation

class AVAudioPlayerHelper
{
    var audioPlayer :AVAudioPlayer?

    var getVolume: Float
    {
        return (audioPlayer?.volume)!
    }

    func increaseVolumeOfAudioPlayer()
    {
        audioPlayer?.prepareToPlay()
        audioPlayer?.play()
    }
}
```

To install Cuckoo, follow these steps:

1. Create your AudioPlayer project with AVAudioPlayerHelper. swift model class and test classes.

2. Install the Cuckoo pod by first running pod init from the command line.

3. Edit the generated podfile and then add Cuckoo as a test target, as shown in Listing 4-2.

4. Run the pod install command.

5. Close the project and reopen the workspace.

6. Click on the Project folder and choose Test Target ➤ Build Phases.

7. Click + and choose New Run Script Phase.

8. Add Listing 4-6 to the Run Script section and change UrlSession.swift to AVAudioPlayerHelper.swift.

9. Build the project.

10. Right-click on AudioPlayerWithCuckooTests and add GeneratorModel.swift to the test folder, similar to Figure 4-1.

11. Using the newly available functions from GeneratorModel. swift, we mock testIncreaseAudioplayerVolume().

In Listing 4-13, we see that in setUp() we create a mock Audio Player and in testIncreaseAudioplayerVolume() we change the volume to max volume. We then assert that we've made that change.

Listing 4-13. Audio Player Mocked Code

```swift
import XCTest
import Cuckoo
import AVFoundation

@testable import AudioPlayerWithCuckoo

class AudioPlayerWithCuckooTests: XCTestCase
{
    var mockAudioPlayer:MockAudioPlayer?
    let maximumVolume:Float = 1.0

    class MockAudioPlayer
    {
        let volume:Float = 1.0
        func getAudioPlayer() -> AVAudioPlayer
        {
            let url = NSURL.fileURL(withPath: Bundle.main.path(forResource:
            "Sample",
                                                                ofType: "mp3")!)

            let _: NSError?
            var tempAudioPlayer: AVAudioPlayer?

            do
            {
                try
                    tempAudioPlayer = AVAudioPlayer(contentsOf: url)
```

```
        } catch
        {
            print("audioPlayer error \(error.localizedDescription)")
        }
        tempAudioPlayer?.volume = volume

        return tempAudioPlayer!


    }
}

override func tearDown()
{
    // Put teardown code here. This method is called after the
    invocation of each test method in the class.
    super.tearDown()
    mockAudioPlayer = nil
}

func testIncreaseAudioplayerVolume()
{
    let mock = MockAVAudioPlayerHelper()
    mockAudioPlayer = MockAudioPlayer()

    let tempAudioPlayer = mockAudioPlayer?.getAudioPlayer()

    stub(mock) {
        (mock) in
        when(mock.audioPlayer.get).thenReturn(tempAudioPlayer)
    }

    stub(mock) {
        (mock) in
        when(mock.increaseVolumeOfAudioPlayer()).thenDoNothing()
    }

    stub(mock) {
        (mock) in
        when(mock.getVolume.get).thenReturn(maximumVolume)
    }

    XCTAssertEqual(mock.audioPlayer?.volume,maximumVolume)
    XCTAssertEqual(mock.getVolume,maximumVolume)
    XCTAssertEqual(mock.audioPlayer?.volume,tempAudioPlayer?.volume)
    XCTAssertNotNil(verify(mock).audioPlayer)
}

}
```

We run the tests; see Figure 4-8 for the test results.

Figure 4-8. AudioPlayerWithCuckooTest results

Summary

This chapter looked at how to use Cuckoo to mock out a basic HelloWorld class, calling a REST API, User Defaults, Dates, and AudioPlayer classes. As yet, there aren't any de facto standards or mocking frameworks to use in Swift and because of its read-only runtime, it may be a while before one emerges. But in the meantime, Cuckoo provides ways to stub or fake out the objects so you can be just as successful in your testing.

CHAPTER 5

UI Testing

iOS apps fail for a number of reasons other than simple logic errors that we typically catch with unit tests. The app may not install correctly, or there may be a problem when you move from landscape to portrait and back again. Your layout also might not work on one of the devices such as the iPad mini that you forgot to test it on. Or it might just hang if the network is down, leaving the user with no option but to close the app.

It's just not possible to test for these conditions using classic unit testing. If you remember the Swift Agile testing pyramid, you need to be at higher up on the pyramid to catch these User Interface or UI errors (see Figure 5-1) for a Swift Agile Pyramid.

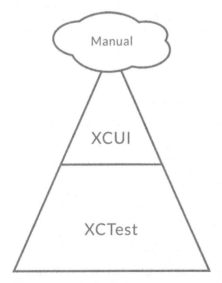

Figure 5-1. *The Swift Agile testing pyramid*

The bulk of your tests should be unit tests—these are small tests at the function level. UI tests are at the top of the pyramid and are harder to maintain. These are typically black box tests where each test creates a new session as we work through the UI to get to the dialog that we're trying to test. So UI tests by their very nature are brittle—small UI changes can break multiple UI tests. Not surprisingly, there are fewer UI tests. But we still need to test the app end to end and not just its isolated components.

© Godfrey Nolan 2017
G. Nolan, *Agile Swift*, DOI 10.1007/978-1-4842-2102-0_5

We're going to have to use the XCUI framework to test our UIs. There are a couple of other options out there, but most of them have been abandoned or deprecated, such as Frank, a Cucumber derivative, or Apple's UIAutomation framework, so XCUI seems to be the logical way to go.

Recording Tests

Recording tests get you started using XCUI. I don't think anyone would use them exclusively for testing as, like all auto-generated tools, they can create a lot of extra garbage code. However it's a great place to start getting your feet wet.

We'll use the Calculator app from the Chapter 5 folder of the book's source code. Open it with Xcode 8 and run the app. If everything is working correctly, you should see the image in Figure 5-2.

| | iPhone 6s – iOS 10.0 (14A5309d) | |
| Carrier 🛜 | 4:27 PM | 🔋 |

0			
7	8	9	/
4	5	6	*
1	2	3	-
0	=	Clear	+

Figure 5-2. *Calculator app*

To add XCUI testing to this or any other project, take the following steps in Xcode:

1. Choose File ➤ New ➤ Target.

2. Scroll down to Test.

3. Choose UI Testing Bundle.

4. Click Next.

5. Click Finish.

If all goes well, you should see a CalculatorUITests folder and a
CalculatorUITests.swift file similar to Figure 5-3.

Figure 5-3. *XCUI template code*

The template code has three methods—setUp(), tearDown(), and testExample().
Note the highlighted red circular button on the bottom of the screen beside the blue
breakpoint arrow. If you don't see that button, you've done something wrong in the steps
and need to try again.

To start recording, put the cursor in the testExample() method and click the red
button to start recording. Try multiplying 3 times 4 and then check the answer in the
results field. See Listing 5-1.

Listing 5-1. Autogenerated XCUI Recorded Code

```swift
func testExample() {

    // Use recording to get started writing UI tests.
    // Use XCTAssert and related functions to verify your tests produce the
    correct results.

    let app = XCUIApplication()
    app.buttons["3"].tap()
    app.buttons["*"].tap()
    app.buttons["4"].tap()
    app.buttons["="].tap()
```

119

```
app.otherElements.containing(.button, identifier:"7").children(matching:
.textField).element.tap()
```

```
}
```

XCUIApplication() creates the app in the simulator. Then we tap the 3, *, 4, and equals buttons. XCUI doesn't seem to understand what we're doing when we click on the results field. But we have enough to get us started. Recording is a great starting point for tests, but don't be surprised if you end up rewriting a lot of the code it produces.

XCUI uses the Accessibility framework, so make sure the text field has a name that it can reference. Click on the Main.storyboard and open the Identity Inspector tab. Choose the result field in the Storyboard and name the Identifier resultsFld, as shown in Figure 5-4.

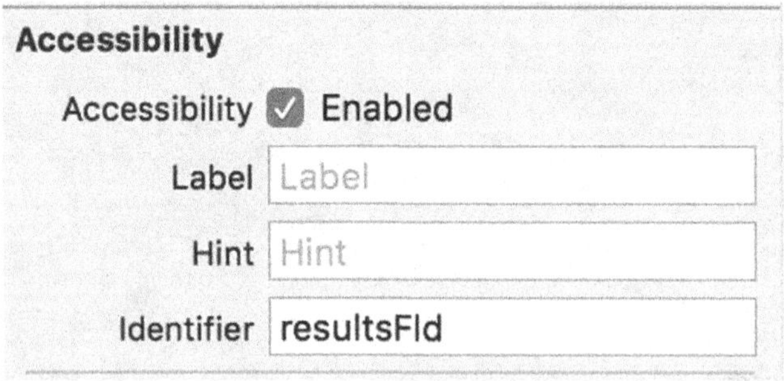

Accessibility

Accessibility ☑ Enabled

Label | Label

Hint | Hint

Identifier | resultsFld

Figure 5-4. *Updating accessibility identifiers*

Like with our unit tests, we want to Arrange-Act-Assert. We've arranged or set up the objects, we've added the numbers, and now we need to assert that the resultsFld displays 12 when we multiply 3 * 4. Using XCTAssert, we can assert that the value in the resultsFld is 12 as follows.

```
XCTAssert(app.textFields["resultsFld"].value! as! String == "12")
```

Update the testExample as shown in Listing 5-2 and run the test again. It should run successfully.

Listing 5-2. Updated Recorded Code

```
func testExample() {

    let app = XCUIApplication()
    app.buttons["3"].tap()
    app.buttons["*"].tap()
    app.buttons["4"].tap()
    app.buttons["="].tap()
```

```
let resultTextField = app.textFields["resultsFld"]
XCTAssert(resultTextField.value! as! String == "12")
```

}

Figure 5-5 shows the output from the reporting tab after the code runs.

Figure 5-5. *XCUI successful test report*

Coded Tests

In the last section you learned how you can use XCUI to record user interface apps. But in most cases you're going to write them from scratch. Recording tests is great but it's usually just used to jumpstart the tests.

There are some very good reasons why you want to consider writing your tests. XCUI recording is an excellent tool but the general consensus from the iOS community is that, to date, it's a step back from the previous UIAutomation Apple and third-party tools that were available in the Objective-C stack.

There are also times when recording the test simply isn't going to work and you're going to have to figure out why. Writing your own tests helps you learn how it all fits together if you need to debug any recorded or handwritten tests. UI tests are very brittle; a simple change in an earlier view can have a ripple effect on later tests and if you don't know how to debug and fix problems, you're going to have to spend a lot of time re-recording your tests.

XCUI also generates the code and like all code-generation tools the generated code is never neat and tidy. It's going to be easier to read your handwritten code than the XCUI generated code if you revisit it sometime in the future. You're also going to need to know how the recording works in case you're testing the wrong thing. There really is no other option; you're still going to need to write your tests.

Component Parts

XCUI has three component parts:

- XCUIApplication
- XCUIElement
- XCUIElementQuery

Using these three components, we can target a single element or a group of elements in your app, create an action for the button or label to use, and then verify that the element responded with the expected result.

We launch the app using XCUIApplication and then use XCUIElementQuery to find the appropriate XCUIElement to test. Once we perform an action on the XCUIElement we can use XCTAssert to test its value.

In most modern automated testing frameworks, we perform the three As when we write our tests. That is, we arrange, act, and assert. So we *arrange* that the app is launched (XCUIApplication) and that we're targeting the correct button or table cell on the correct view (XCUIElementQuery); we *act,* meaning we perform an act such as tap on the button or enter some text in a text field (XCUIElement); and then we *assert* (XCTAssert) or test that the button or text field is in the expected state after we've performed our action.

XCUIApplication

XCUIApplication creates a new instance of your application by calling XCUIApplication().launch(). Every test runs in a separate process so that you can guarantee that the app is always beginning in the same fresh, unblemished state. If there's another process running, it will be killed before the new application or process starts.

XCUIElementQuery

Each element on a view can be an XCUIElement type, such as a button or a cell or an identifier such as a label or title. In order to interact it with it, we need to identify it. We do this using XCUIElementQuery.

You can search for buttons, labels, titles, text fields, and table cell elements directly using its name or using elementAtIndex(i). If you're searching by name, as you saw earlier, you're going to need to make sure every element has its accessibility information filled in. This seems to be a win-win as not only does it help with the XCUI testing, it also makes your app easier for visually impaired users to use. Table 5-1 shows some examples of calling some common elements.

Table 5-1. *XCUIElementQuery Examples*

Assertion Type	Description
Text field	`XCUIApplication().textFields["Full Name"]`
Button	`XCUIApplication().buttons["Check Validations"]`
Button	`XCUIApplication().buttons.elementBoundByIndex(0)`
Label	`XCUIApplication().staticTexts["Two Words Needed"]`
Table	`XCUIApplication().tables.element.cells.` `elementBoundByIndex(4)`

Each XCUIElementQuery() needs to filter down the choices to a unique element or elements. If the query isn't exact, then the test will fail and you won't be able to perform any actions. You can also chain your XCUIElementQueries to make the query more obvious; for example, XCUIApplication().tables.element.cells["Call Mom"]. buttons["More"].

Finally, you can also use matching predicates such a BEGINSWITH or ENDSWITH to filter the list of elements. For example, the following will find a label or labels that end with Football Club.

```
let soccerTeams = NSPredicate(format: "label ENDSWITH 'Football Club'")
```

XCUIElement

Once we have the correct XCUIElement, we can perform an action and assert that the action produced the correct response.

We can tap a button as follows:

```
app.buttons.elementBoundByIndex(1).tap()
```

Or enter text in a text field:

```
emailTextField.tap()
emailTextField.typeText("email@email.com")
```

Click a link on a WebView:

```
app.links["Soccer"].tap()
```

See if a label or title exists:

```
staticTexts["Burton Albion"].exists
```

123

Sample Test

We can code the earlier recorded example from scratch following the three As—arrange, act, and assert. Now that we've explained how XCUI recording works under the hood, the XCUI commands should make a lot more sense.

Arrange

We showed how to create a UI target in the last blog. Using our sample code from Chapter 5, go ahead and create the UI target again. We can reuse the setUp() code that the recording process generated, which is shown in Listing 5-3. This will start the app and create the context.

Listing 5-3. XCUIApplication

```
class CalculatorUITests: XCTestCase {

    override func setUp() {
        super.setUp()

        // stop if any test fails
        continueAfterFailure = false

        // start the app
        XCUIApplication().launch()
    }
}
```

Act

The app has been created, so we need to act next. For us that's as simple as multiplying two numbers. Connect to the XCUIApplication context and then tap on the appropriate XCUIElement buttons to create the actions we need to multiple the two numbers. We are once again borrowing from our earlier example. See Listing 5-4.

Listing 5-4. Acting on the XCUIElement Buttons

```
func testExample() {

    let app = XCUIApplication()
    app.buttons["3"].tap()
    app.buttons["*"].tap()
    app.buttons["4"].tap()
    app.buttons["="].tap()

}
```

Assert

Finally, we assert that the result is what we expect. We need to use XCUIElementQuery to gain access to the text field, which we've named resultsFld, so that we can find the text field at app.textFields["resultsFld"].

It's pretty straightforward to test that the value is 12 using XCTAssert:

```
XCTAssert(app.textFields["resultsFld"].value! as! String == "12")
```

CLI

One of our requirements throughout the book is to be able to run tests outside of Xcode. If you install the command-line tools (assuming you're running Xcode 8.x), then the following command will run the test from the command line.

```
xcodebuild test -project Calculator.xcodeproj -scheme Calculator
-destination 'platform=iOS Simulator,name=iPhone 6s,OS=9.3'
```

Reporting

Xcode does a very good job of reporting on the XCUI test results. Figure 5-6 shows the test results for a working UI test, including all the intermittent steps.

Figure 5-6. *Test results for the working XCUI test*

It's also worth getting familiar with the logs. Figure 5-7 shows the condensed version of the logs for a working test.

125

Figure 5-7. *Logs for the working XCUI test*

Clicking on the expander icon at the method level shows an expanded version of the captured logs, as shown in Figure 5-8.

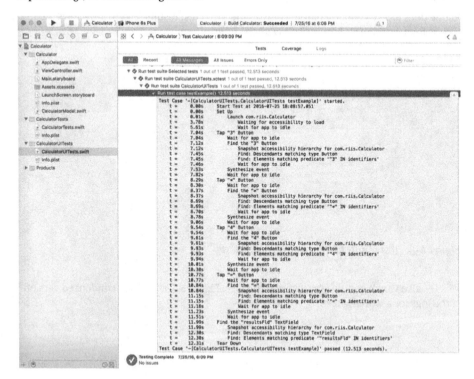

Figure 5-8. *Expanded logs for working XCUI test*

If you want to see the actual log files, expand the Writing Diagnostic Log section. See Figure 5-9.

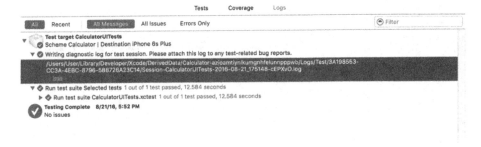

Figure 5-9. *Location of log files*

It's unlikely that you're going to spend much time looking at the logs when the tests pass. Figure 5-10 shows a failing test.

```
func testExample() {

    let app = XCUIApplication()
    app.buttons["3"].tap()
    app.buttons["*"].tap()
    app.buttons["4"].tap()
    app.buttons["="].tap()

    let resultTextField = app.textFields["resultsFld"]
    XCTAssert(resultTextField.value! as! String == "11")

}

}
```

Figure 5-10. *Failing test in Xcode*

The test reports are excellent at showing what step failed; see Figure 5-11.

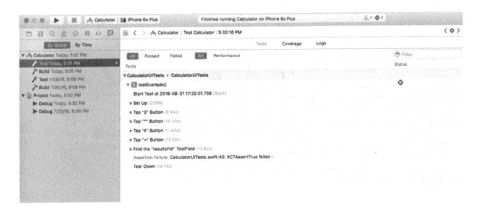

Figure 5-11. *Failing test in reporting*

Figure 5-12 shows the failing test in the logs.

Figure 5-12. *Failing test in logs*

The expanded logs can be very helpful when you're trying to debug your XCUIElementQuery logic and can't figure out why you're testing the wrong XCUIElement or why it's not resolving to a single XCIElement (see Figure 5-13).

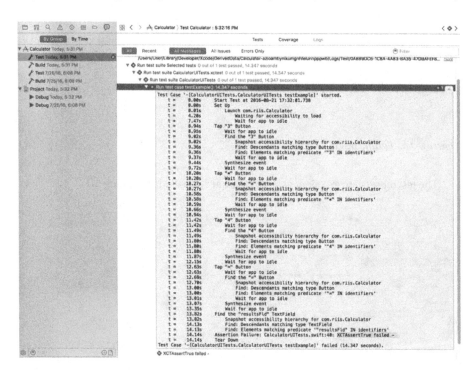

Figure 5-13. *Expanded logs*

Summary

You should not expect to be writing as many XCUI tests as XCTests in your application, but XCUI testing is a crucial part of your Agile Swift testing pyramid. Remember that unit tests are at the method level, which is inside-out testing, whereas XCUI is used to test the flow of your application, which is more of an outside-in type of testing.

CHAPTER 6

Test Driven Development

It wouldn't be right in a book about Agile development if we didn't make an effort to show Test Driven Development (TDD) in action. So in this chapter we're going to create an app from scratch using our TDD approach. The sample app we're going to create using TDD will be for a daily horoscope. I'm not a fanatic about astrology by any means, but it's a simple app that will allow us to show our TDD techniques in action.

Understanding Test Driven Development

TDD means that we take the first feature on our list of features and code using the following process:

- Write a test first and see it fails (red)

- Write the simplest possible solution to get the test to pass (green)

- Refactor to remove any code smells (refactor)

Then we take another feature from the list and repeat the red/green/refactor process. We repeat this process until all the features are completed.

■ **Note**   In classic TDD, whether it's in Java or C#, we don't usually have to worry about any infrastructure. But things aren't that straightforward in iOS. When we create a Swift class to test, we often have to create a Storyboard that will display or interact with that Swift class. So when we say write the simplest possible solution to get the unit test to pass, that will also have to include some iOS Storyboard code too. Alternatively, you can leave that to the refactoring stage if you like, but it just needs to be completed somewhere in the red/green/refactor process.

© Godfrey Nolan 2017
G. Nolan, *Agile Swift*, DOI 10.1007/978-1-4842-2102-0_6

Unit Testing versus TDD

So far we've been focused on unit testing our Swift apps. But unit testing is not necessarily TDD. Test Driven Development involves writing the unit test before writing the code, whereas unit tests don't mandate when you write tests. Without TDD, more often than not unit tests are written at the end of a coding cycle to improve code coverage metrics. So you can do unit testing with TDD, but you can't do TDD without unit testing. Once you start TDD, you should find that it is less painful than classic unit testing.

Value of TDD

We know that unit testing and testing in general helps catch mistakes, but why would we want to use TDD? There are several fundamental reasons for this. TDD pushes the developer to only implement what is minimally needed to implement a feature, so it can help us shape our design to actual or real use and avoids any gold plating in our implementation. We call this process YAGNI, or You Ain't Going to Need It. It leads to much simpler implementations as the focus is on what is required, not necessarily what you might be able to do so saving money and reducing complexity.

In these days of faster mobile startups, YAGNI also encourages getting a minimum viable product or MVP out the door as quickly as possible. The business owners choose the bare minimum of features needed to launch an app in the app store. This minimum feature list is then split into manageable chunks that feed your developers' TDD process.

Unit testing without TDD can get you a regression test suite that will help you from introducing any defects as your code. But because you're writing unit tests before you write any code, your understanding of what the code is trying to do is naturally going to be much fresher than writing unit tests weeks or even months later. The TDD regression test suite is probably going to have more coverage and be much more comprehensive than unit testing without TDD.

Also because of the ongoing refactoring, the code becomes more maintainable and much leaner, leading to a longer life for your codebase. It is very easy to write horrible, untestable code in Swift. Refactoring will encourage you to write single-line methods that are easily tested rather than monolithic View Controllers.

Finally, the process of coding in this continuous red/green/refactor cycle helps kill procrastination, as the focus is on small discrete steps and the app gradually emerges from the bottom up as one feature after another is implemented.

Writing an App Using TDD

Before we get started, we're going to need some basic requirements for our horoscope app.

- Display each star sign
- Display information about each star sign
- Display a daily horoscope for star sign

There are lots of other things that we could add, but we're practicing YAGNI so we're going to go with the minimum of features for our MVP horoscope app.

We're going to create a simple horoscope app that displays the list of Zodiac signs, displays some information about each star sign, and then shows the daily horoscope.

Feature 1

The initial feature requires that we display a list of star signs, which we will do using a Table View, as shown in Figure 6-1.

Figure 6-1. *Horoscope app feature 1*

Getting Started

For this feature, we need to create a new project. Close any other Xcode projects that you have open. Because of the nature of the mobile apps we not only need to create a Swift file with our horoscope information, but we also need to set up the interface to display the signs.

Note that while this will end up being a Master-Detail application, the TDD process tells us that we only need the minimum amount of information to create our feature. A single view application meets our immediate needs (see Figure 6-2).

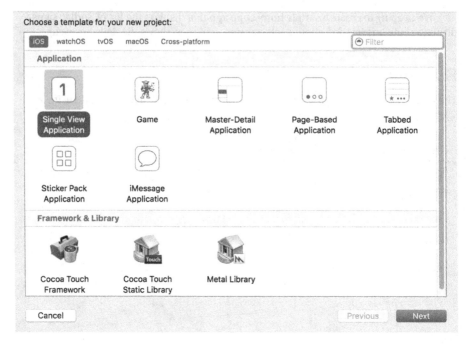

Figure 6-2. *Single view iOS application*

1. In Xcode, go to File ➤ New ➤ Project.

2. User iOS and Application, choose the Single View Application template, as shown in Figure 6-2.

3. Click next and enter the following options (see Figure 6-3):

    •   Product Name: Horoscope

    •   Organization Name: Example

    •   Organization Identifier: com.example

    •   Language: Swift

    •   Devices: iPhone

    •   Include Unit Tests: Checked

4. Click Next.

5. Navigate to Desktop ➤ Agile Swift ➤ Chapter 6.

6. Check Create Git Repository on My Mac.

7. Click Create.

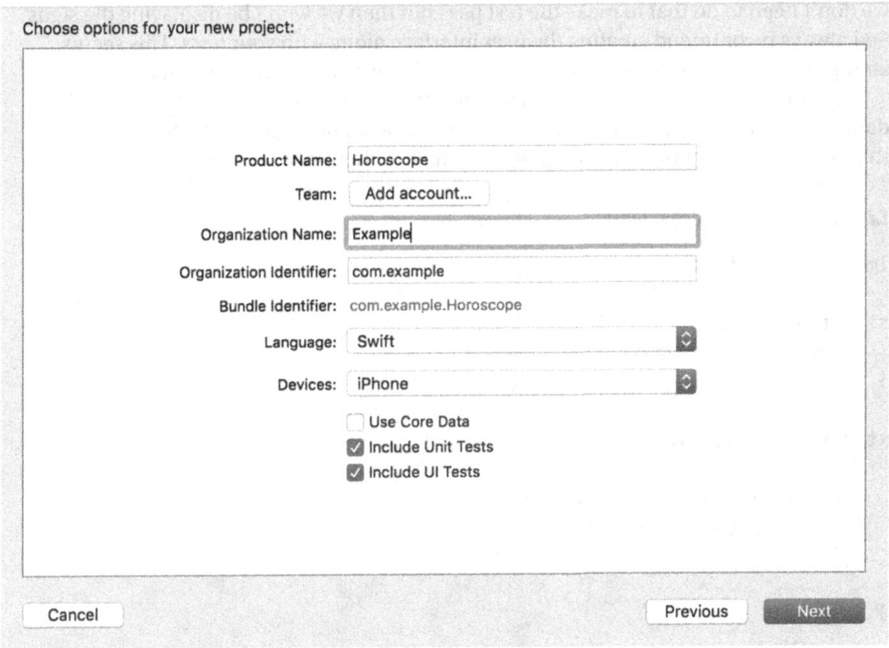

Figure 6-3. *Use these project options*

Writing the Test First

Open the HoroscopesTests.Swift file in the HoroscopesTest folder. It will be the same template we've seen in the past, with setUp, tearDown, testExample, and testPerformanceExample methods. Our first feature is to display the horoscope star signs, not the first page. Create the unit tests in Listing 6-1 to start the process.

Listing 6-1. Feature 1 Unit Tests

```
let horoscopeModel = HoroscopeData.horoscopes

func testNumHoroscopeSigns() {
      XCTAssertEqual(horoscopeModel.count, 12)
}

func testFirstHoroscopeSignAries() {
    XCTAssertEqual(horoscopeModel[0].name, "Aries")
}
```

A couple of things to note. Because we haven't created the horoscope data this isn't going to compile. So we're going to need to create a struct or a class to store the horoscope data. Secondly we're going to need to create the user interface too. Technically we don't need to do that to make the test pass but then we won't be displaying the signs. So I always recommend creating the user interface along with your tests. This seems strange in the world of TDD, but there really isn't any way around it for mobile apps.

Listing 6-2 shows the code in HoroscopeData.swift. We can use a struct, as the data isn't going to change and nobody is going to be adding, editing, or deleting any of the elements of our horoscope data once we have it then way we want.

Listing 6-2. Horoscope Data

```
import Foundation

struct Horoscope {
    var name: String
}

struct HoroscopeData {

    static let horoscopes = [
        Horoscope(name: "Aries")
    ]

}
```

We've done enough for the tests to compile and run. Run the tests by clicking on the test icon ✅ in the HoroscopeTests class. The testNumHoroscopeSigns should fail, as shown in Figure 6-4.

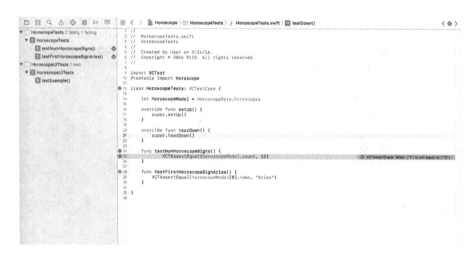

Figure 6-4. *Failing tests feature 1*

To get the tests to pass, add the rest of the horoscope names to the `HoroscopeData. swift` file, see Listing 6-3.

Listing 6-3. Complete List of Horoscope Signs

```swift
import Foundation

struct Horoscope {
    var name: String
}

struct HoroscopeData {

    static let horoscopes = [
        Horoscope(name: "Aries"),
        Horoscope(name: "Taurus"),
        Horoscope(name: "Gemini"),
        Horoscope(name: "Cancer"),
        Horoscope(name: "Leo"),
        Horoscope(name: "Virgo"),
        Horoscope(name: "Libra"),
        Horoscope(name: "Scorpio"),
        Horoscope(name: "Sagittarius"),
        Horoscope(name: "Capricorn"),
        Horoscope(name: "Aquarius"),
        Horoscope(name: "Pisces")
    ]

}
```

Run the tests again and this time they should pass, as shown in Figure 6-5.

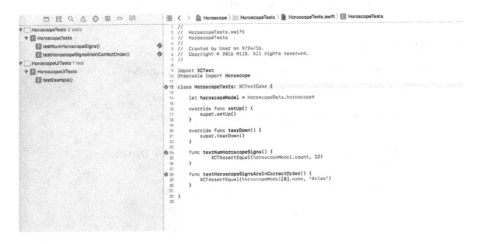

Figure 6-5. *Passing tests feature 1*

We've created the data for our app, but it's not much use without the user interface. So we're going to create that next.

Creating a Table View App

1. In the Project Navigator, notice that there are a number of files created automatically. Xcode created a View Controller as well as an AppDelegate.swift file when we chose the single view application.

2. Click on Main.storyboard.

3. Click on the View Controller in the Document Outline. If it's not visible, then click the Show Document Outline button ▮▯ at the bottom left of the Editor area.

4. Click on the View Controller and delete it.

5. Delete ViewController.swift.

6. Go to the Object Library ⊙ at the bottom right of the Xcode screen.

7. In the search window, search for the Table View Controller in the object window.

8. Drag and drop a Table View Controller onto the Editor.

9. Click on the Table View Controller in the Document Outline window.

10. Next, click on the Attributes Inspector ▼ in the Inspector area.

11. Check on the Is Initial View Controller to make this the Storyboard Entry point when the application is started.

Adding a Label

1. In the Document Outline, expand Table View Controller.

2. Click on Table View.

3. In the Utilities area on the right, go to the Attributes Inspector ▼.

4. Under Table View, from the Content menu, choose Dynamic Prototype.

5. In the Document Outline, expand the Table View.

6. Expand the Table View Section.

7. Click the remaining table view cell to select it.

8. In the Attributes Inspector, set the Style menu to custom.

9. Enter signCell in the Identifier just below the Style

10. In the Document Outline, expand Table View Cell and click on Content View.

11. Go to the Object Library ⊡ at the bottom right of the Xcode screen.

12. In the search window, search for the Label in the object window.

13. Drag and drop the Label on the Table View Cell in the Storyboard, see Figure 6-6.

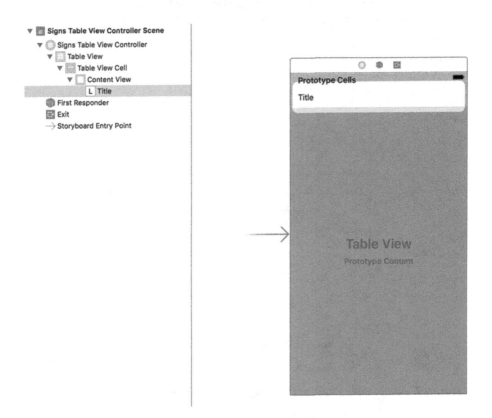

Figure 6-6. *Adding a Label to the Signs Table's Table View Cell*

Creating a Table View Class

1. Go to File ➤ New ➤ File.

2. On the left, under iOS, make sure Source is selected.

3. Choose Cocoa Touch Class.

4. From the Subclass of menu, choose UITableViewController.

5. Edit the name of the Class to be SignsTableViewController (see Figure 6-7).

6. Click Next.

7. You should already be in the Horoscope folder, so click Create.

8. Notice that SignsTableViewController.swift has been added to the Project Navigator.

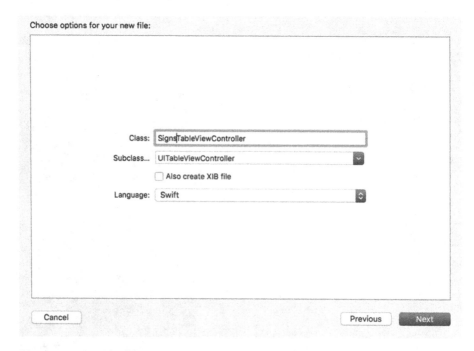

Figure 6-7. *Create Table View Controller SignsTableViewController*

By making our class a subclass of the UITableViewController, we will have a SignsTableViewController.swift class with template methods for all the functionality we need for our table object.

Connecting the Table Class

1. In the Project Navigator, click on Main.storyboard.

2. In the Document Outline, click Table View.

3. In the Utilities area on the right, click on the Connections inspector tab ⊕.

4. Notice there are two outlets that are assigned to the Table View: dataSource and delegate.

5. Next we need to connect the view we have in the Storyboard to our new class. In the Document Outline, click Table View Controller.

6. In the Utilities area on the right, click the Identity Inspector tab 📄.

7. Next to Class, type SignsTableViewController or choose it from the dropdown.

8. Click Return to apply the change.

9. In the Document Outline, click Table View.

10. In the Utilities area on the right, click the Connections Inspector tab ⊕ again.

11. Notice that dataSource and delegate are now connected to the Signs Table View Controller (see Figure 6-8).

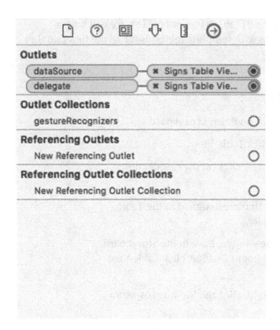

Figure 6-8. *dataSource and delegate outlets*

Now we can start adding the code we need to populate the table cells.
We need to make the following changes to `SignsTableViewController.swift`:

- Add a reference to the horoscope data by adding `let horoscopeModel = HoroscopeData.horoscopes`

- Edit the `numberOfSectionsInTableView`, set to `return 1` as there is only one section table

- Edit the `numberOfRowsInSectionsInTableView` to `return horoscopeModel.count` i.e. 12 signs

- Configure the cell to display the horoscope data

- Change

```
    let cell = tableView.dequeueReusableCell(withIdentifier:
"reuseIdentifier", for: indexPath)
```

to

```
let cell = tableView.dequeueReusableCell(withIdentifier: "signCell", for:
indexPath)
```

And add the cell name so it can be displayed.

```
let horoscopeDetail = horoscopeModel[indexPath.row]
cell.textLabel?.text = horoscopeDetail.name
```

The cleaned up file is shown in Listing 6-4.

Listing 6-4. Table View Code

```
import UIKit

class SignsTableViewController: UITableViewController {

    let horoscopeModel = HoroscopeData.horoscopes

    override func viewDidLoad() {
        super.viewDidLoad()
    }

    override func didReceiveMemoryWarning() {
        super.didReceiveMemoryWarning()
    }

    override func numberOfSections(in tableView: UITableView) -> Int {
        return 1
    }

    override func tableView(_ tableView: UITableView, numberOfRowsInSection
    section: Int) -> Int {
        return horoscopeModel.count
    }

    override func tableView(_ tableView: UITableView, cellForRowAt
    indexPath: IndexPath) -> UITableViewCell {
        let cell = tableView.dequeueReusableCell(withIdentifier: "signCell",
        for: indexPath)

        // Configure the cell...
        let horoscopeDetail = horoscopeModel[indexPath.row]
        cell.textLabel?.text = horoscopeDetail.name
        return cell
    }
    /*
    // MARK: - Navigation
    // In a storyboard-based application, you will often want to do a little
        preparation before navigation override func prepare(for segue:
        UIStoryboardSegue, sender: Any?) {
```

143

```
    // Get the new view controller using segue.
       destinationViewController.
    // Pass the selected object to the new view controller.
  }
  */

}
```

We need to leave the template prepare function in our code as we're going to need it in the next feature. Run the app and the table displays with the 12 signs.

Refactor

The final stage of testing is to refactor. Begin by deleting the `ViewController.swift` file. Right click and choose delete and then choose 'Move to Trash.' The remaining code is so simple we don't need to do much refactoring with the code. We should, however, add more tests to make sure all the remaining signs are being displayed, as shown in Listing 6-5.

Listing 6-5. Adding more Tests

```
func testHoroscopeSignsAreInCorrectOrder() {
    XCTAssertEqual(horoscopeModel[0].name, "Aries")
    XCTAssertEqual(horoscopeModel[1].name, "Taurus")
    XCTAssertEqual(horoscopeModel[2].name, "Gemini")
    XCTAssertEqual(horoscopeModel[3].name, "Cancer")
    XCTAssertEqual(horoscopeModel[4].name, "Leo")
    XCTAssertEqual(horoscopeModel[5].name, "Virgo")
    XCTAssertEqual(horoscopeModel[6].name, "Libra")
    XCTAssertEqual(horoscopeModel[7].name, "Scorpio")
    XCTAssertEqual(horoscopeModel[8].name, "Sagittarius")
    XCTAssertEqual(horoscopeModel[9].name, "Capricorn")
    XCTAssertEqual(horoscopeModel[10].name, "Aquarius")
    XCTAssertEqual(horoscopeModel[11].name, "Pisces")

}
```

Feature 2

In feature 2, we want to display information about each sign. Let's keep it basic so we can choose to display the following information:

- Name
- Description
- Symbol
- Month

We'll display the information on a second view when the user clicks on the relevant table cell.

We could store the information in a SQLite database, but that's not a requirement, so we'll take the YAGNI route and instead store the sign information in our `struct`. It's neat, clean, and meets the requirement.

Writing the Test

Start with the tests. We can quickly test for the Description, Symbols, and Month in the `HoroscopeTests.swift` file, as shown in Listing 6-6.

Listing 6-6. Testing Description, Symbol, and Month

```swift
func testHoroscopeDescription() {
    XCTAssertEqual(horoscopeModel[0].description, "Courageous and
    Energetic.")
}

func testHoroscopeSymbols() {
    XCTAssertEqual(horoscopeModel[0].symbol, "Ram")
}

func testHoroscopeMonth() {
    XCTAssertEqual(horoscopeModel[0].month, "April")
}
```

To get the tests to run, we need to add the description, symbol, and month to the horoscope struct in `HoroscopeData.swift` (see Listing 6-7).

Listing 6-7. Updated Horoscope Struct

```swift
struct Horoscope {
    var name: String
    var description: String
    var symbol: String
    var month: String
}
```

Run the tests. As expected, seeing as we're in the red part of the red/green/refactor TDD cycle, the unit tests all fail (see Figure 6-9).

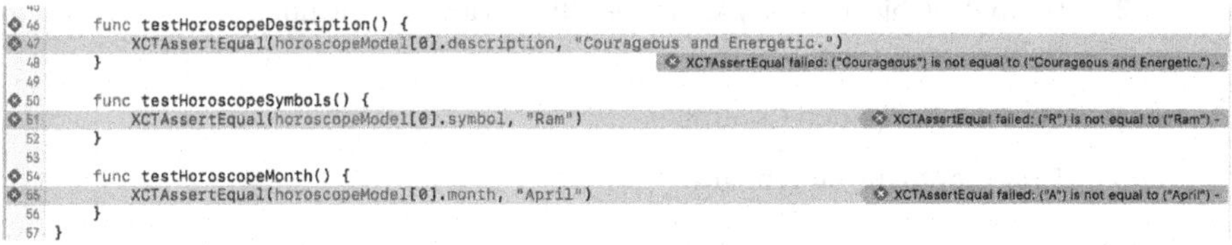

Figure 6-9. Failing tests

145

Complete the description of the Aries horoscope data shown in Listing 6-8.

Listing 6-8. Completed Horoscope Details for Aries

```
struct HoroscopeData {

    static let horoscopes = [
        Horoscope(name: "Aries",
        description: "Courageous and Energetic.",
        symbol: "Ram",
        month: "April")
    ]
}
```

Run the tests again and they turn green, as shown in Figure 6-10.

```
46    func testHoroscopeDescription() {
47        XCTAssertEqual(horoscopeModel[0].description, "Courageous and Energetic.")
48    }
49
50    func testHoroscopeSymbols() {
51        XCTAssertEqual(horoscopeModel[0].symbol, "Ram")
52    }
53
54    func testHoroscopeMonth() {
55        XCTAssertEqual(horoscopeModel[0].month, "April")
56    }
57 }
```

Figure 6-10. *Passing tests*

Creating a User Interface

We're not done yet, as we need to display the information to the user. We're going to create a detailed view of the horoscope sign. When the user clicks on one of the signs it will take them to a detail view of the information for that sign. To add this functionality to our app, we'll first add a Navigation Controller.

Adding the Navigation Controller

1. In the Project Navigator, click on Main.storyboard.

2. Hide the Document Outline button by clicking the ▣ at the bottom left of the Editor area.

3. Go to the Object Library ⊚ in the Utilities area on the bottom right.

4. Find the Navigation Controller.

5. Drag it onto the Storyboard.

6. The Navigation Controller comes with two scenes:

    - Navigation Controller: Manages the relationships and transitions between our views

    - Root View Controller: The first controller instantiated by the Navigation Controller

7. Delete the provided Root View Controller so the Table View Controller can be the first controller instantiated.

8. Click onto the top bar of the Root View Controller so that it is outlined in blue and delete it.

The Editor should now look similar to what you see in Figure 6-11.

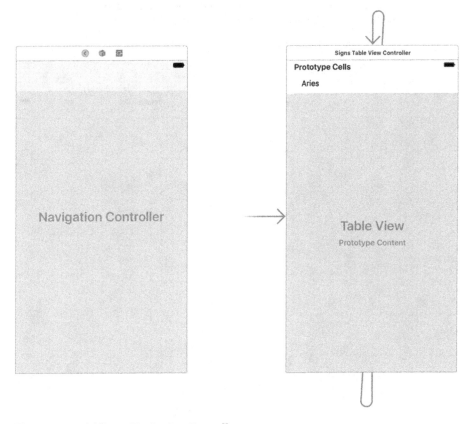

Figure 6-11. *Adding a Navigation Controller*

Setting the Initial View Controller

We can see the gray arrow is pointing to our Signs Table View Controller. We need to change that so that the Navigation Controller is our initial View Controller.

1. Open the Document Outline button by clicking the ■ at the bottom left of the Editor area.

2. Click on the Navigation Controller to select it.

3. In the Utilities area on the right, click on the Attributes inspector tab ⬇.

4. In the View Controller section, check on Is Initial View Controller.

5. In the Editor area, the gray arrow should now be pointing to the Navigation Controller, as shown in Figure 6-12.

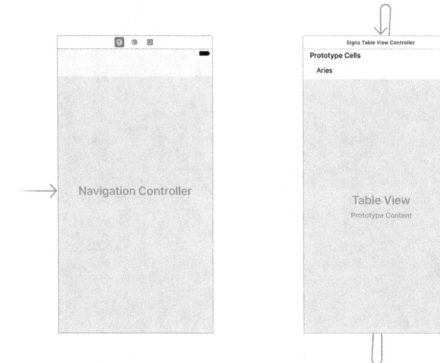

Figure 6-12. *Initial View Navigation Controller*

Setting the Root View Controller

Next we need to set the Signs Table View Controller as the root View Controller so it is the first controller that users see. We set this in the Connections Inspector.

1. Select the Navigation Controller in the Editor.

2. In the Utilities area on the right, click on the Connections Inspector tab ⊖.

3. In the Triggered Segues section in the Connections Inspector tab, click on the root View Controller.

4. Hold Ctrl and drag from the + circle beside root View Controller to the Signs Table View Controller.

5. In the Connections Inspector tab ⊖ the root View Controller is now connected to the Signs Table View Controller.

6. In the Editor section, the Signs Table View Controller is now the root View Controller for the Navigation Controller, as shown in Figure 6-13.

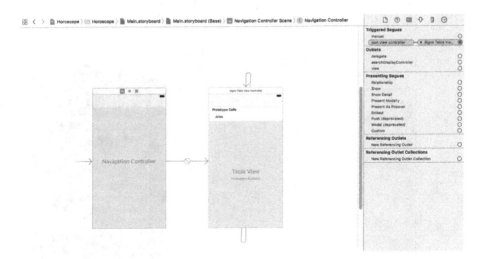

Figure 6-13. *Setting the root View Controller*

This now creates a connection between the Navigation Controller and the Table View Controller which is now the Root View Controller for the Navigation Controller.

Adding the Detail View Controller

Next we create a View Controller to display the sign information and then create a connection between it and the cell in our Signs Table View Controller. Therefore, when users tap on the cell, they are taken to the new View Controller.

1. We need to add a View Controller that will list the details about our star sign. In the Object Library, ⊡ find the View Controller.

2. Drag a View Controller and drop it to the right of Signs Table View Controller in the Editor.

3. Hold Ctrl and drag from the Label 'Aries' cell to the View Controller on the right.

4. A Segue menu will open, as shown in Figure 6-14. Under Selection Segue, click Show.

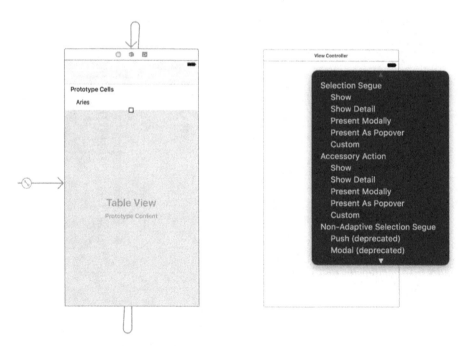

Figure 6-14. Creating the segue between the Table View and View Controller

5. In the Document Outline, expand Signs Table View Controller if it isn't already expanded.

6. Click on Navigation Item to select it.

7. In the Utilities area on the right, click the Attributes Inspector tab ⊝.

8. Enter Signs as the Title.

9. The Signs Table View Controller title bar has been updated.

10. Click the Run button and you should be able to click on a Sign and get a blank detail page.

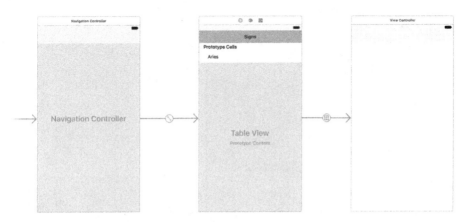

Figure 6-15. *Adding the Detail View Controller*

Adding a Name, Description, Symbol, and Month

We can quickly create the layout for the View Controller that appears when you tap on a horoscope sign. This view will list the extra information we created earlier.

1. Go to the Document Outline. If it's not open, click on ▣.

2. Under View Controller Scene in the Document Outline, click View Controller to select it.

3. In the Object Library area on the right, ⊙ search for Label.

4. Add a Label for Name, Symbol, Month, and Description, and then order them as shown in Figure 6-16.

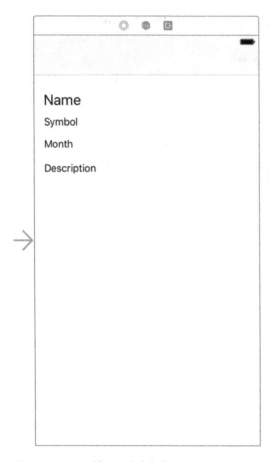

Figure 6-16. *Adding info labels to the Detail View Controller*

Creating SignsDetailViewController Class

1. Go to File ➤ New ➤ File in the Project Navigator.

2. Make sure on the left, under iOS, that Source is selected.

3. Double-click Cocoa Touch Class to choose it.

4. From the Subclass of menu, choose UIViewController.

5. Choose SignsDetailViewController as the name of the class, see Figure 6-17.

6. Click Next and Create.

7. In the Project Navigator, click on Main.storyboard.

8. In the Document Outline, select Signs Detail View Controller.

9. In the Utilities area on the right, click on the Identity Inspector tab 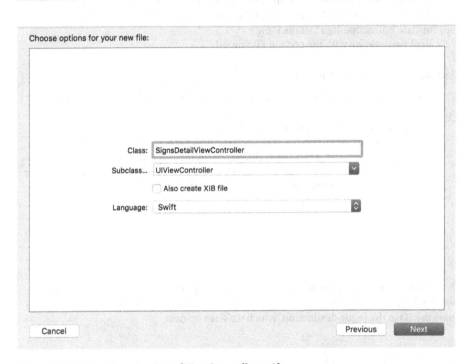.

10. For the class, select SignsDetailViewController from the drop-down then press Return. SignsDetailViewController is now connected to the new class.

■ **Note** Just like with UITableViewController, by subclassing UIViewController, our new class will have template code for the view functionality we're going to need.

Choose options for your new file:

Class:	SignsDetailViewController
Subclass...	UIViewController
	Also create XIB file
Language:	Swift

Cancel   Previous   Next

Figure 6-17. *Creating SignsDetailViewController.swift*

Creating a Segue

Add a variable for the current sign at the start of the detail view, as shown in Listing 6-9.

Listing 6-9. Adding the currentSignDetail Variable

```
class SignsTableViewController: UITableViewController {
    var currentSignDetail:Int?
```

Uncomment the prepare method under // MARK: - Navigation; see Listing 6-10.

Listing 6-10. Preparing for Segue Code

```
// MARK: - Navigation

// In a storyboard-based application, you will often want to do a little
preparation before navigation
override func prepare(for segue: UIStoryboardSegue, sender: Any?) {
    // Get the new view controller using segue.destinationViewController.
    // Pass the selected object to the new view controller.
}
```

Segues allow us to pass data from one page to the next. In this case we're going to send the ID of the table cell that's been clicked so that we can pick this up and display the appropriate horoscope sign Details View.

Replace the code with the code in Listing 6-11.

Listing 6-11. Updated prepareForSegue

```
override func prepare(for segue: UIStoryboardSegue, sender: Any?) {

    if (segue.identifier == "showDetail") {
        if let indexPath = tableView.indexPathForSelectedRow {
            let signsDetailViewController:SignsDetailViewController =
                    segue.destination as! SignsDetailViewController
            let signNumber = indexPath.row
            signsDetailViewController.currentSignDetail = signNumber

        }
    }
}
```

We're preparing for the segue by first referencing the showDetail segue, and then we're taking the indexPath.row or the ID of the clicked row and using the signNumber to pass the ID to the segue destination, which we'll set up next.

Creating the showDetail Segue

Let's connect the two views so showDetail knows where to go.

1.   Click on Main.storyboard.

2.   In the Editor, click on the segue between the Table View and Detail View Controllers (see Figure 6-18).

3.   Click the Attributes Inspector tab ⬇.

4.   Enter showDetail in the Identifier field so that the prepare method knows where to send the data.

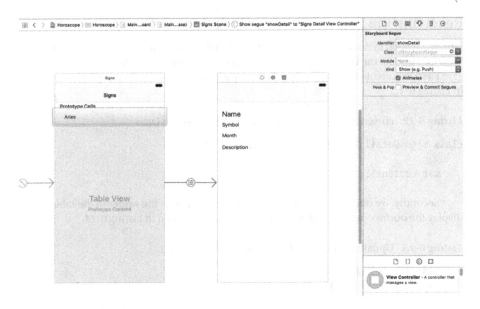

Figure 6-18. showDetail Segue

Connecting Sign Detail Outlets

1. Click on `Main.storyboard` in the Project Navigator.

2. Hide the Document Outline by clicking ▣ .

3. Click the top bar of the Signs Detail View Controller in the Editor area.

4. Click on the Assistant Editor button ⊘ to view the Storyboard next to `SignsDetailViewController.swift`.

5. Hold Ctrl and drag the Name label to the `SignsDetailViewController.swift` file.

6. In the menu that pops up, set the following:

   - Connection: Outlet

   - Name: signName

   - Type: UILabel

   - Storage: Weak

7. Click Connect.

8. Repeat this process for `signSymbol`, `signMonth`, and `signDescription`.

Receiving the Segue Data and Updating the Detail View

Finally we need to do two things—receive the data that's been passed from the Sign Table View and update the labels with the horoscope information for that sign.

First, let's create the currentSignDetail variable to receive the segue data, as shown in Listing 6-12.

Listing 6-12. currentSignDetail Variable for Receiving Segue Data

```
class SignsDetailViewController: UIViewController {

    var currentSignDetail:Int?
```

Secondly, we update the viewDidLoad method to change the values of the labels and display the horoscope information from our struct, as shown in Listing 6-13.

Listing 6-13. Update Labels with the currentSignDetailValue

```
override func viewDidLoad() {
    super.viewDidLoad()

    if let currentSignDetailValue =  currentSignDetail
    {
        signName.text = HoroscopeData.horoscopes[currentSignDetailValue].
        name
        signSymbol.text = HoroscopeData.horoscopes[currentSignDetailValue].
        symbol
        signMonth.text = HoroscopeData.horoscopes[currentSignDetailValue].
        month
        signDescription.text = HoroscopeData.horoscopes[currentSignDetailVa
        lue].description
    }
}
```

Refactor

When we run the app the Description is getting truncated, see Figure 6-19.

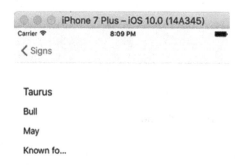

Figure 6-19. *Truncated Sign Description*

156

We can fix this as follows.

1. Click on the Main.storyboard

2. Click on Description field on the Signs Detail View Controller

3. In the Utility Area open the Attributes Inspector ⬇

4. Set Lines = 0

5. Go to Line Break and choose Word Wrap.

6. Open the Size Inspector ▤

7. Set X = 15, Y = 200, Width = 300 and Height = 75

Run the simulator again and the Description is no longer truncated.

You can also remove the unused template methods in the views as well as add more tests similar to what was shown in the last step. Removing the unused code will make the remaining code more obvious when you return in the future and you can find the template code again if needed.

Feature 3

Feature 3 says we should display the horoscope for each star sign. Once again, let's start with the testing. The requirement is that it must be free and available in XML or JSON (Java Script Object Notation). We can create our own simple API or use one of the many free APIs. In this case, we're going to use the daily horoscope from http://www.findyourfate.com/rss/dailyhoroscope-feed.asp.

The Aries output can be seen in Listing 6-14.

Listing 6-14. Horoscope XML

```
<rss version="2.0">
  <channel>
      <title>Daily Horoscope</title>
      <description>Daily Horoscopes by FindYourFate.com</description>
      <link>http://www.findyourfate.com</link>
      <item>
          <title>Aries Horoscope for Thursday, September 29, 2016</
title>
              <description>
                      You may feel that you are in a crucial place in your
                      life today, but try not to let your emotions run
                      away with you. It is easy to blame others, but you
                      know that will not be the answer. Try not to hurt
                      someone`s feelings today when they try to give you a
                      compliment. Flattery is not your thing, but speaking
                      out loud about what you are thinking may not be
                      the best way to handle this. Don`t discard those
```

```
                invitations just yet. Such events can be fun and you
                could finally meet that special someone.
        </description>
        <link>
                http://horoscope.findyourfate.com/
                ariesdailyhoroscope.html
        </link>
    </item>
  </channel>
</rss>
```

We know from our unit testing chapter that we're not going to test any network communication. It is not something we want to do during our unit testing. But we should be testing our own methods that call findyourfate. Listing 6-15 shows a test to see if we appended the URL correctly.

Listing 6-15. testAppendURL

```swift
func testAppendURL() {
    let compURL = HoroscopeService.sharedInstance.appendURL(sign: "Aries")
    XCTAssertEqual(compURL, "http://www.findyourfate.com/rss/dailyhoroscope-
    feed.asp?sign=Aries&id=45")
}
```

The appendURL code is shown in Listing 6-16.

Listing 6-16. AppendURL

```swift
func testAppendURL() {
    let compURL = HoroscopeService.sharedInstance.appendURL(sign: "Aries")
    XCTAssertEqual(compURL, "http://www.findyourfate.com/rss/dailyhoroscope-
    feed.asp?sign=Aries&id=45")
}
```

Run the code and the test passes.

Creating the User Interface

We want to display the horoscope on our Detail View so that it can take the FindYourFate daily horoscope and display it to our users.

Updating the Detail View

1. Click on the Main.storyboard.

2. Go to the Object Library ⊙ and find the Label object.

3. Drag and drop the label onto the Signs Detail View Controller and put it under the description, as shown in Figure 6-20.

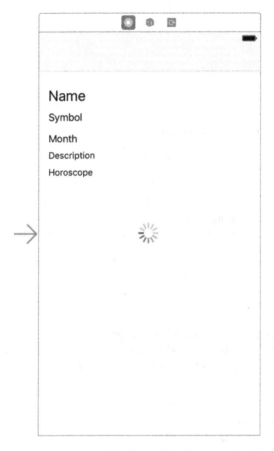

Figure 6-20. *Completed signs detail view*

Creating the Horoscope Service

1. Open File ➤ New ➤ File.

2. Create a `.swift`.

3. Cut and paste the code in Listing 6-17. appendURL is the code we tested and `callDailyhoroscopeApi` is template code for calling an URL asynchronously.

Listing 6-17. HoroscopeService.swift

```swift
import Foundation

class HoroscopeService
{
    static var horoscopeUrl:String = ""

    class var sharedInstance :HoroscopeService
    {
        struct Singleton
        {
            static let instance = HoroscopeService()
        }

        return Singleton.instance
    }

    func appendURL (sign:String) -> String {
        let baseURL = "http://www.findyourfate.com/rss/dailyhoroscope-feed.asp"
        let findYourFateID = "45"
        let completedURL = baseURL + "?sign=" + sign + "&id=" +
        findYourFateID
        return completedURL
    }

    func callDailyhoroscopeApi(sign:String,parameters: AnyObject?,
                        success: (( _ resp: Data) -> Void)?,
                        failure: (( _ error: NSError? ) -> Void)?)
    {

        let urlString = appendURL(sign: sign)
        let url = URL(string: urlString)
        let request = NSMutableURLRequest(url: url!)
        let session = URLSession.shared
        request.httpMethod = "GET"
        request.addValue("application/xml", forHTTPHeaderField: "Content-
        Type")
        request.addValue("application/xml", forHTTPHeaderField: "Accept")

        let task = session.dataTask(with: request as URLRequest,
        completionHandler:
            {
                data, response, error -> Void in
                let httpResponse = response as! HTTPURLResponse
                let strData = NSString(data: data!, encoding: String.
                Encoding.utf8.rawValue)
                print("Body: \(strData)")
```

```
            if httpResponse.statusCode == 200
            {
                DispatchQueue.main.async(execute: { () -> Void in
                    success!(data!)
                })
            }
            else
            {
                DispatchQueue.main.async(execute: { () -> Void in

                    failure!(error as NSError?)
                })
            }
        })
        task.resume()
    }
}
```

Updating SignsDetailViewController.swift

There are three things we need to do to update the Horoscope field.

- Call HoroscopeService's callDailyhoroscopeApi method to get the horoscope

- Parse the returned XML to pull out the daily horoscope field, Description

- Finally, update the Horoscope field with the daily horoscope

The complete code is shown in Listing 6-18.

Listing 6-18. SignsDetailViewController

```
import UIKit

class SignsDetailViewController: UIViewController, XMLParserDelegate {

    var currentSignDetail:Int?

    @IBOutlet weak var signName: UILabel!
    @IBOutlet weak var signSymbol: UILabel!
    @IBOutlet weak var signMonth: UILabel!
    @IBOutlet weak var signDescription: UILabel!
    @IBOutlet weak var signHoroscope: UILabel!
    @IBOutlet weak var spinner: UIActivityIndicatorView!
```

```swift
var parser = XMLParser()
var element = NSString()

var horoscopeDescription = String()
var insideAnItem = false

// MARK: - View life cycle

override func viewDidLoad() {
    super.viewDidLoad()

    if let currentSignDetailValue =  currentSignDetail
    {
        signName.text = HoroscopeData.horoscopes[currentSignDetail
        Value].name
        signSymbol.text = HoroscopeData.horoscopes[currentSignDetail
        Value].symbol
        signMonth.text = HoroscopeData.horoscopes[currentSignDetail
        Value].month
        signDescription.text = HoroscopeData.horoscopes[currentSign
        DetailValue].description

        self.callDailyhoroscopeApi(sign: HoroscopeData.horoscopes
        [currentSignDetailValue].name)
    }
}

override func didReceiveMemoryWarning()
{
    super.didReceiveMemoryWarning()
    // Dispose of any resources that can be recreated.
}

// MARK: - API Call
func callDailyhoroscopeApi(sign:String)
{
    self.spinner.startAnimating()
    HoroscopeService.sharedInstance.callDailyhoroscopeApi(sign: sign,
    parameters: nil, success: {
        (data) in

        self.spinner.stopAnimating()

        self.parseXmlData(data: data)

        }) { (error) in
            self.spinner.stopAnimating()
    }
}
```

```swift
// MARK: - XMLParser
func parseXmlData(data:Data)
{
    //create xml parser
    self.parser = XMLParser(data: data)
    self.parser.delegate = self
    self.parser.parse()

    let success:Bool = self.parser.parse()
    if success {
        print(success)
    }
}

// MARK: - XMLParser Delegate methods

// didStartElement
func parser(_ parser: XMLParser, didStartElement elementName: String,
namespaceURI: String?, qualifiedName qName: String?, attributes
attributeDict: [String : String])
{

    element = elementName as NSString
    if (elementName as NSString).isEqual(to: "item")
    {
        insideAnItem = true
        print(attributeDict)
    }
}

// foundCharacters
func parser(_ parser: XMLParser, foundCharacters string: String)
{

    if element.isEqual(to: "description") && insideAnItem == true
    {
        print("description is \(string)")
        self.horoscopeDescription =    string

    }
}

// didEndElement
func parser(_ parser: XMLParser, didEndElement elementName: String,
namespaceURI: String?, qualifiedName qName: String?)
{

}
```

```
func parserDidEndDocument(_ parser: XMLParser)
{
    DispatchQueue.main.async {
        self.spinner.stopAnimating()
        //Display the data on UI

        self.signHoroscope.text =   self.horoscopeDescription
    }

}

}
```

Figure 6-21 shows the final app, complete with the displayed Aries horoscope from findyourfate.com. To refactor the code we would probably add some URL mocking to the test using the http connection example Cuckoo library example that we explored in Chapter 4.

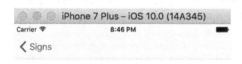

Aries

Ram

April

Courageous and Energetic.

Over the next few weeks, you will want to get to the bottom of certain financial matters at the moment and will keep digging in your heels until certain people come clean. It is a time for negotiating, looking for compromises and fairer deals all round. You will be handling discreet information well, attracting secrets from others without even appearing to ask. OK, so at times you will also express yourself too forcibly. With Mercury in the deepest area of your chart, you will feel strongly about certain situations, and will not easily change your mind.

Figure 6-21. *Aries detail page with the daily horoscope*

I would be the first to admit that creating the user interface gets in the way of creating a red/green/refactor cadence when you're developing. The unit testing code is limited to code that doesn't directly relate to the iOS UI framework. Ideally we wouldn't have to open Xcode at all and use the command line tools such as xcodebuild to build our app. While that isn't realistic at the moment there are a number of 3rd party tools that can help limit the amount of time we have to spend using Storyboards and the Interface Builder.

We looked at the Stevia library for building interfaces in Chapter 3. There are a number of Swift DSLs (Domain Specific Languages) such as Stevia and SnapKit that aim to dramatically shorten the lines of User Interface code in your applications.

Listing 6-19 shows the Detail View Page code written in Stevia that we wrote for a final refactoring stage.

Listing 6-19. Stevia version of the SignsDetailView

```
import UIKit
import Stevia

class SignsDetailView: UIView
{
    var signName = UILabel()
    var signSymbol = UILabel()
    var signMonth = UILabel()
    var signDescription = UILabel()
    var signHoroscope = UILabel()
    var spinner = UIActivityIndicatorView()

    convenience init()
    {
        self.init(frame:CGRect.zero)
        // This is only needed for live reload as injectionForXcode
        // doesn't swizzle init methods.
        render()
    }

    func render()
    {
        backgroundColor = .white
        spinner.color = .darkGray
        signName.font = UIFont.boldSystemFont(ofSize: 18)

        sv(
            signName,
            signSymbol,
            signMonth,
            signDescription,
            signHoroscope,
            spinner

        )
```

```
layout(
    100
    |-10-signName-10-| ~ 30,
    8,
    |-10-signSymbol-10-| ~ 30,
    8,
    |-10-signMonth-10-| ~ 30,
    8,
    |-10-signDescription-10-|,
    8,
    |-10-signHoroscope-10-|,
    |-spinner-|
)

    self.signDescription.style(self.labelStyle)
    self.signHoroscope.style(self.labelStyle)

}
func labelStyle(l:UILabel)
{
    l.numberOfLines = 0
    l.textAlignment = .left
    l.lineBreakMode = .byWordWrapping
    l.textColor = .black
    l.text = NSLocalizedString("Description", comment: "")
}
}
```

Instead of using the Interface Builder to drag and drop the Labels we can do all of that in code, see the Layout below for each of the fields.

Listing 6-20. SignsDetailView layout

```
layout(
    100,
    |-10-signName-10-| ~ 30,
    8,
    |-10-signSymbol-10-| ~ 30,
    8,
    |-10-signMonth-10-| ~ 30,
    8,
    |-10-signDescription-10-|,
    8,
    |-10-signHoroscope-10-|,
    |-spinner-|
}
```

The layout is created in the loadView() SignsDetailViewController as follows, see Listing 6-21.

Listing 6-21. Inflating the SignsDetailView layout

```
let signsDetailView = SignsDetailView()

override func loadView() {
    view = signsDetailView
}
```

As Swift 3 matures hopefully more libraries will emerge that will allow developers to spend more time writing model code and less time connecting interfaces. The complete Stevia example is available with the rest of the source code online.

Conclusion

In this chapter we created a simple three feature Horoscope app using Test Driven Development or TDD.

Index

© Godfrey Nolan 2017
G. Nolan, *Agile Swift*, DOI 10.1007/978-1-4842-2102-0

■ **T**

■ U, V, W

Get the eBook for only $4.99!

Why limit yourself?

Now you can take the weightless companion with you wherever you go and access your content on your PC, phone, tablet, or reader.

Since you've purchased this print book, we are happy to offer you the eBook for just $4.99.

Convenient and fully searchable, the PDF version enables you to easily find and copy code—or perform examples by quickly toggling between instructions and applications.

To learn more, go to http://www.apress.com/us/shop/companion or contact support@apress.com.

Printed in the United States
By Bookmasters